"Chaintanyam shashvatam shantam
vyomatitam nirjanam,
Naad bindu kalatitam tasmai
shri guruvai namah."

The one who is the supreme soul, the one who is eternally peaceful, the one who is beyond the limits of the sky, the one who is beyond the past, the one who is beyond all desires, and the one who is beyond sound and art, we salute such a noble guru.

Religion and Spirituality

Goswami Tulsidas
- ❑ Sri Ramcharitmanasa (Doha- Chopai in Hindi, Roman Description in English) 1500.00

Ed. Acharya Bhagwan Dev
- ❑ Sanskar Vidhi 125.00

B.K. Chaturvedi
- ❑ Gods & Goddesses of India 150.00
- ❑ Shiv Purana 95.00
- ❑ Vishnu Purana 95.00
- ❑ Shrimad Bhagvat Purana 75.00
- ❑ Devi Bhagvat Purana 75.00
- ❑ Garud Purana 75.00
- ❑ Agni Purana 75.00
- ❑ Varah Purana 75.00
- ❑ Brahamvevart Purana 75.00
- ❑ The Hymns & Orisons of Lord Shiva (Roman) 30.00
- ❑ Sri Hanuman Chalisa (Roman) 30.00
- ❑ Pilgrimage Centres of India 95.00
- ❑ Chalisa Sangreh 40.00

S. K. Sharma
- ❑ The Brilliance of Hinduism 125.00
- ❑ Sanskar Vidhi (Arya Samaj) 125.00

Dr. B.R. Kishore
- ❑ Hinduism 95.00
- ❑ Rigveda 60.00
- ❑ Samveda 60.00
- ❑ Yajurveda 60.00
- ❑ Atharvveda 60.00
- ❑ Mahabharata 60.00
- ❑ Ramayana 60.00
- ❑ Supreme Mother Goddeses Durga (4 Colour Durga Chalisa) 95.00

Manish Verma
- ❑ Fast & Festivals of India 95.00

Prof. Gurpret Singh
- ❑ Soul of Sikhism 125.00

Shiv Sharma
- ❑ Soul of Jainism 125.00

Pt. Ramesh Tiwari
- ❑ Shrimad Bhagavad Gita (Krishna, the Charioteer) (Sanskrit, Hindi, English & Description in English) 400.00

Manan Sharma
- ❑ Buddhism (Teachings of Buddha) 150.00
- ❑ Universality of Buddha 150.00

Anurag Sharma
- ❑ Life Profile & Biography of Buddha 150.00
- ❑ Thus Spoke Buddha 150.00

Udit Sharma
- ❑ Teachings & Philosophy of Buddha 150.00

S.P. Ojha
- ❑ Sri-Ram-Charit Manas 95.00

Chakor Ajgaonkar
- ❑ Realm of Sadhana (What Saints & Masters Say) 30.00

K.H. Nagrani
- ❑ A Child from the Spirit World Speaks 10.00

F.S. Growse
- ❑ Mathura & Vrindavan, The Mystical Land of Lord Krishna (8 Colour photos) 495.00

Dr. Giriraj Shah
- ❑ Glory of Indian Culture 95.00

R.P. Hingorani
- ❑ Chalisa Sangreh (Roman) 60.00

Acharya Vipul Rao
- ❑ Srimad Bhagwat Geeta (Sanskrit & English) 75.00

Dr. Bhavansingh Rana
- ❑ 108 Upanishad (In press) 150.00

Eva Bell Barer
- ❑ Quiet Talks with the Master 60.00

Joseph J. Ghosh
- ❑ Adventures with Evil Spirits 80.00

Dr. S.P. Ruhela
- ❑ Fragrant Spiritual Memories of a Karma Yogi 100.00

Yogi M.K. Spencer
- ❑ Rishi Ram Ram 100.00
- ❑ Oneness with God 90.00

H. Seereeram
- ❑ Fundamentals of Hinduism 250.00

Books in Roman
- ❑ Bhajan, Lokgeet or Aartiyan (Roman English, Hindi) 95.00
- ❑ Hindu Vrat Kathayen (Including Saptvaar Vrat Kathayen) 40.00
- ❑ Chalisa Sangreh (Including Aarties in Roman) 60.00
- ❑ Shri Satya Narayana Vrat Katha (In English and Hindi) 25.00
- ❑ Sanatan Dharm Pooja 95.00
- ❑ Sudha Kalp 95.00
- ❑ Shiv Abhisek Poojan 25.00
- ❑ Daily Prayer (Hindi, English, French, Roman) 25.00
- ❑ Sanatan Daily Prayer 25.00
- ❑ Durga Chalisa 10.00
- ❑ Gaytari Chalisa 10.00
- ❑ Shiv Chalisa 10.00
- ❑ Hanuman Chalisa 10.00

Acharya Vipul Rao
- ❑ Daily Prayer 25.00

Books can be requisitioned by V.P.P. Postage charges will be Rs. 20/- per book. For crders of three books the postage will be free.

DIAMOND POCKET BOOKS

X-30, Okhla Industrial Area, Phase-II, New Delhi-110020, Phone : 011-51611861, Fax : 011-51611866
E-mail : sales@diamondpublication.com, Website : www.fusionbooks.com

Navrattan Bodh Katha

A discourse on the epic 'Navrattan Bodh'
(The Nine Jewels of Realisation) by
Shri Vallabhacharya ji

Discourse by
His Holiness Shri Kirit 'Bhai ji'

Translated by
Preetipal

Transcribed by
Mrs. (Dr.) Shashi Prabha Tomar
Tulsi Parivaar
(Bareilly)

DIAMOND BOOKS

ISBN : 81-288-1000-6

Publisher
Diamond Pocket Books (P) Ltd.
X-30, Okhla Industrial Area,
Phase-II, New Delhi-110020
Phone : 011-51611861-865
Fax: 011-51611866
E-mail : sales@diamondpublication.com
Website : www.diamondpublication.com

Edition : 2005

Price : 95/-

Printed at : Adarsh Printers, Shahdara, Delhi-32

Navrattan Bodh Katha **Rs. 95/-**
by Shri Vallabhacharya ji

PARAM PUJYA GURUDEV

**"Vasudev sutam devam,
Kansa chanur mardanam.
Devaki paramanandam,
Krushnam vande jagadgurum."**

To dispel the darkness of ignorance and nescience, a divine embodiment of Love, Truth and Beauty, appeared amidst us on 21st July, 1962 in Porbundur (Gujarat). Today, He is known to the world as Parampujya Kirit Bhaiji.

Gurudev's discourses provide spiritual succour and nourishment to all the seekers. Embellished with references, anecdotes and analogies drawn from our ancient scriptures, such as–The Upanishads, Vedas, Shrimad Bhagvatam, Bhagvad Geeta and the Ramayana–Gurudev's 'pravachans' are like a nectarean drink, served to parched souls. The profound and sublime principles which are presented in our 'granths' and 'shastras', are enunciated, simplified and served to all the 'saadhaks'.

A seeker feels encouraged to tread on the path of Truth and Realisation, revealed in our scriputures. Gurudev's voice rings-out-loud:

"YOU CAN DO IT! YOU WILL DO IT!
AND YOU WILL SUCCEED!"

Gurudev's teachings depict the triple confluence of KARMA, BHAKTI and GNAN (duty, devotion and knowledge). He inspires the aspirants to perform their duties, enthusiastically!

"Tasmaat utishtha!" ***(Bhagvad Geeta)***

"Therefore, get up and fight!"

He shows the proper way:

"Tadvidhi pranipaten pariprashnen sevaya!"

"Go to the enlightened souls, bow down and humbly put forth your questions. Serve them!"

He explains the mysteries and sublime–truth pertaining to the soul, the super-soul, knowledge, illusion, detachment and devotional service. (The *'Ram-Geeta'*)

He reveals the path of pure love, selfless-service and complete surrender, through His discourses on the '*Narad Bhakti Sutra*' and '*Shri Madhurashtakam*'.

The tears of love and separation, which shed profusely from the eyes of all the '*saadhaks*' attending His discourses, are a proof of the divine-bliss, which the soul experiences after a communion with Him–The *Paramatma*!

We are all blessed, to have received the shelter of the lotus-feet of our Guruji.

**"Dhyan mulam gururmurti,
Pooja mulam gurur padam.
Mantra mulam gurur vaakyam,
Moksha mulam gurur krupa.**

* * *

SHRI VALLABHACHARYA JI

*　　　　*　　　　*

• **Birth :** In 1478 A.D. (Vik. Sam. 1535), Vallabhacharya (later known as Mahaprabhuji) was born in the sacred forest of Champaranya near Raipur in Madhya Pradesh (Central India) to a brahmin couple, Shri Laxman Bhatt ant Illama garu. Shri Laxman Bhatt was the descendant of Yagnanarayan Bhatt, to whom the Lord had promised on the completion of a 100 Somayagnas that the Lord himself would be born in his family. At the time of His birth, there was a great threat from Mughal rulers attacking the region. So when Vallabh was born, the parents were passing through the forests of Champaranya. Illanguru gave birth to a still-born, premature baby. Believing this baby to be dead they abandoned it below a tree and proceeded further. On their way to South India, the couple had a dream that GOD was calling them back in that baby form. The couple went back to that place and they found that there was a fire protecting the baby from the wild animals of the forest. The mother stepped into the fire to take baby Vallabh.

• **Baby Vallabh awarded the title "Jagadguru":** As a child, Vallabh was extremely intelligent. He mastered the essence of the Vedas and other scriptures at the tender age of 11. His theory of Brahmvad was challenged by Mayavadists during his tour of Indian holy places at the age of 11. Vallabh's first step towards the successful intoduction of his Pushti philosophy was in the court of King Krishnadevaraya of Vijayanagar in south India where a long debate was taking place on questions such as, whether the world is real or imaginary, who is the creator of this world? No any philosopher had satisfying answers or explanations. At such a crucial time, Sri Vallabhacharya entered the court and within seven days, gave satisfactory replies to all the challenging queries and that too with scriptural evidence. All the pundits (scholars) became speechless in front of him and gave their full consent to His theory of 'Shuddhadwaita Brahmavada'. These scholars also, awarded him with a title of 'Jagadguru', a great teacher of the universe. The king gave 700 gold coins to Acharya Shri Vallabh. Just like in today's time, the wealth was a danger in terms of keeping you away from God therefore Vallabh kept only seven coins for the gold shringars (ornaments) for the shrine.

• **Ashtakshara Mahamantra:** When Shri Vallabhacharya was on a visit to northwest India, the Lord requested him to come to Mount govardhan to meet Him. Asking people around Mt. govardhan, Vallabh found that there was one cow going to the mountain everyday and releasing milk at a certain place. Vallabh asked people to dig that area. At that time the Lord revealed Himself to Shri Vallabh in the form of Shree Nathji. At this time, the Lord hugged Shri Vallabhacharya and gave him the sacred mantra "Shree Krishna: Sharnam Mama" to initiate people.

• Pushtimarg, the path of divine grace is based on the 'Shudhadvaita' philosophy, initially shown by Shri Vallabhacharya. Shri Vallabh strongly suggested that Lord Shree Krishna is the ultimate, Krishna is everything and everything is Krishna. Thus Shri Krishna's blessing alone and only can free humans from the painful cycle of birth and death.

• Shree Vallabhacharya wrote many books, but many of them are not available today due to lack of proper preservance. Many important books/articles/padas written by Shri Vallabhacharya and the Acharyas of Vallabhkul are still available and famous in vaishnava society. Yamunashatakam, Navaratnam and many other padas, and Subodhiniji book are very important for Vaishnavas to read and understand.

The philosophy of Sri Vallabhacharya is Shuddha-Advaita or pure monism, because he does not admit Maya like Sankara, and believes that the whole world of matter and souls is real and is only a subtle form of God. Those who bring Maya for the explanation of the world are not pure Advaitins, because they admit a second to Brahman. Shri Vallabhacharya ji holds that Brahamn can create the world without any connection with such a principle as Maya, but Sankara traces the universe to Brahman through the power of Maya. Hence the philosophy of Shri Vallabhacharya ji is called pure monism or Shuddhadvaita. Vallabha expounded that system in the Anu-Bhashya, his commentary on the Brahma Sutras. He called it Shuddha-Advaita or pure monism. Shri Vallabhacharya ji was a Telugu Brahmin of South India. He migrated to the north and developed the views of Vishnuswamin who belonged to the thirteenth century. His system of thought is known by the name Brahma-Vada. Shri Vallabha says that the entire universe is real and is subtly Brahman. The individual souls and the world are, in essence, one with Brahman. Jiva, Kala (time) and Prakriti or Maya are eternal existences, but they have no separate existence apart from Brahman.

Shri Vallabha was a great Sanskrit scholar. He settled down first at Mathura and then at Varanasi. He preached with great zeal the Vaishnava cult and philosophy. He was the founder of the great Vaishnava Muths of Rajasthan and Gujarat. His followers are found in great numbers in Nathdwara.

• **Improtant Works:** Shri Vallabhacharya ji accepts the authority not only of the Upanishads, the Bhagavad-Gita and the Brahma Sutras, but also of the Bhagavata Purana. The important works of Shri Vallabha are Vyasa-Sutra Bhashya (Anu-Bhashya), Jaimini Sutra Bhashya, Bhagavata-Tika Subodhini, Pushti-Pravaha-Maryada and Siddhanta-Rahasya. All these books are in Sanskrit. He has written many books in Braj Bhasha also. The scriptures are the final authority for Vallabha. ***Stress on Worship and Grace*** Vallabha's religion is a religion addressed to the worship of Vishnu in the form of Krishna. It is centred round the conception of a personal and beneficent God who is Sat-Chit-Ananda. Lord Krishna is the highest Brahman. His body consists of Sat-Chit-Ananda. He is called Purushottama.

Vallabha's followers worship Bala-Krishna (Krishna as a baby). They have Vatsalya-Bhava (the attitude which regards God as a child.) Vallabha lays great stress on Pushti (grace) and Bhakti (devotion). Maha-Pushti is the highest grace or Anugraha which helps the aspirants to attain God-realisation.

* * *

PREFACE

Shri Vallabhacharya ji has revealed the path of total surrender to Lord Shri Krishna, in His 'Navrattan-Bodh' or 'The Nine Jewels of Realisation'. The doubts and worries which assail a disciple's mind are wiped away by the benevolent Sadguru.

A devotee sails through the nine forms of devotional-service (NAVDHA BHAKTI) to achieve the ultimate destination–serving the lotus-feet of Lord Shri Krishna. If service is contaminated with 'ego' and 'attachment', then it loses its purity. A servants' sole concern is the happiness and satisfaction of his Lord and master. His 'Dharma' is Shri Krishna's service. His 'Arth' is Shri Krishna's name. His 'Kaam' is Shri Krishna's 'darshan', and his 'Moksh' is 'belonging' to Shri Krishna!!

Complete self surrender unto his Lord and Master!!

Shri Krishna sharanam mama
Shri Krishna sharanam mama
Shri Krishna sharanam mama.

* * *

INDEX

1. Parampujya Gurudev–An Introduction V
2. Shri Vallabhacharya ji–An Introduction Vii
3. Preface Xi
4. Navrattan Bodh Katha 13
5. Chapter 1 14
6. Chapter 2 35
7. Chapter 3 58
8. Chapter 4 78
9. Chapter 5 96
10. Chapter 6 111
11. Chapter 7 122
12. Chapter 8 135
13. Glossary 144

* NAVRATTAN BODH KATHA *

A discourse on the epic 'Navrattan Bodh'
(The Nine Jewels of Realisation)

✻ CHAPTER-I ✻

Shrimad Vallabhacharya says-

"Chinta kapi na karya niveditambh kadapiti,
Bhagwanapi pushtistho na karishyati laukikim chagatim."

–First couplet

The Almighty Shri Krishna, the best amongst all men, the son of Nand and Yashoda, born of Vasudeva and Devki, the beloved of the 'gopis,' (cowherd's daughters, who graze cows) the great lover, when shows boundless love towards the souls gives birth to great souls like Shri Vallabhacharya on this earth. As has been described by the devotees and the thinkers, he gives birth to such great souls like Shri Vallabhacharya to have pity on the human souls, to attract the souls towards himself, and to give a demonstration of his ceaseless generosity, "**Lokvattu lila kevalyam**" (Meaning, he has created this drama of the world only for the benefit of the people). He gives birth to such great souls as Shri Vallabhacharya to take the souls, which have become separated from God, to their destination. As Goddess Sarawati and Lord Brahma, word and meaning, the mountains and coolness, spark and fire, the Sun and ray are inseparable; similarly soul and God are inseparable since time immemorial. Due to this unbreakable relationship, God sends the human beings into the drama of the world that he has created where the consciouseness of the human beings has to fight constantly to not succumb to worldly desires. Human beings forget their real self due to their slavery to the senses and their physical body. Actually, there is an inseparable relation between the soul and God, which can never diminish. But, still for those people who have become separate from God due to their worldly desires, for them, as a father makes many plans to get his separated son back, similarly God also sends his special people on the earth to bring back the souls who are his sons and daughters and to make the souls realise their true self. He also makes the souls realise what is the Supreme Being, why should we surrender completely before God? What is the benefit of worshipping God? Those people who after coming into this world think worldly desires to be everything, to make them think about afterlife, to make them attain God, to make them realise the special place of God in everyone's life, great men like Acharya Vallabhacharya are born.

The great Shri Vallabhacharya has created sixteen epics. The fifth epic of these was 'Siddhant Rahasya'–'The Mysteries of the Principles' on which we have already had a discourse. In 'Mysteries of the Principles' the soul had surrendered everything it had to the Lord. The world is a blessing for a person who has dedicated not only his property, his family, his resources, but his body, his senses, his mind, and his heart to the Lord. Then, the question arises in the mind which has dedicated itself to the Lord that how should this mind that has been offered to the Lord be used.

The sixth epic of Acharya Ji is 'Navrattan Bodh'. **"The wealth of knowledge that is hidden in the hearts of the great men, opens by the questions of the disciples."** It may be in the form of curiosity, it may be in the form of doubts, but till the disciple does not question the master, till then how will the master answer. The speaker may have intelligence and knowledge, but till there is no audience who sits before him, till then what will the speaker speak? 'Navrattan Bodh' has been created because after surrendering everything to God, the nature of the human beings is to worry. The mind and brain abide by logic. The mind thinks. **"To think about the world is to worry."** Those people who are thinking about the world, the society, the family, that is nothing but worry. God has promised at many places through his words, "**You don't worry. If you think about me, I will worry about you.**" The rest is the nature of human beings. He will think. If he thinks, the mind does not accept. If the mind does not accept, the heart indulges in questioning. Whatever this mind decides, it thinks about it. Human ego also acts on what the mind has thought. The minds of the worldly men and the sages also think a variety of different thoughts. Is what I am doing right? Will the Lord accept what service I have done for him? What can I do for the Lord? What does the Lord expect from me? All these questions are nothing but worry.

It is the morning time. Acharya Vallabhacharya Maharaj is walking on the pure Brijbhumi (place where Lord Krishna lived). The disciples are with him. Lucky is the one who gets such company. Due to the company of great men, the mind and the heart become pure. When the mind and the heart become pure, then the thoughts of the mind become pure. When the mind has pure thoughts, it will do good works. If you go into the company of great men, then as Patanjali Maharaj has said – **Ahimsa pratishthayam tatsnigdho vairtyagah** (Meaning, on the establishment of non-violence, the feeling of enemity is suppressed.) When our mind is peaceful, it will think good thoughts. So, when you go into the company of great men, remember –

"**A great man is one on having whose company, we are coloured with the colours of devotion, and our thoughts turn without any effort towards God. If the feeling of enemity is removed from our mind, then we should think that this is a special person sent by God.**" The Acharya is walking in Brajbhumi with his followers – **"Shri Krishna sharanam mam, Shri Krishna sharnam mam, Shri Krishna sharnam mam."** (Meaning, I have gone into the shelter of Shri Krishna). The guru is sitting in the holy piligrimage place of Brijbhumi. What should we say about Brij? "**Brijnath vyapt iti Brij.**" (Meaning, the place where the lord of Brij lives, that is Brijbhumi). Brij means the place of holy discourses, where the mind is engrossed in devotional songs. When a positive feeling comes in the mind, then one should worship God. Madhusudan Saraswati Maharaj has said in 'Bhakti Rasayan' – "**Anukulen bhakti, pratikulen mukti**." The Brijbhumi in which God himself had walked barefoot, that Brijbhumi still exists. In the mountains, in the branches of trees, in the Yamuna, in the groves of trees, there is no place where Radha-Krishna don't dwell. If you go to Brij, go there with the feeling that I will not come back without seeing Radha-Krishna. There should be obstinacy in love. Like sometimes the children and women show obstinacy, similarly the devotee should also have that kind of obstinacy. The guru is giving the religious discourse, **"On singing devotional songs, the hold of worldly desires becomes weaker. On singing devotional songs, all the sins of the past lives are destroyed. On singing devotional songs, one is able to realise God and one gets infinite peace. So sing, Shri Krishna sharnam mam, Shri Krishna sharnam mam, Shri Krishna sharnam mam."**

God has given this order to Arjun in Gita also. Arjun is fighting the war. "This problem of society, this problem of family, these worldly duties, these Bhishmas, these Drons, and these Duryodhans are standing. O Lord, how should I devote myself to you when all these are standing in front of me?" Then, the Lord said, "For devotion, you don't need the body, only the mind. O Arjun! keep this mind in my feet – **"Tasmat sarveshu kaleshu mam anusmar."** (Meaning, if you do not become detached from me for even a moment, then these battles will seem like a song.) The struggle of life is a poem, its music, its bliss, its the butter, and its the sweetness of life.

The great devotee Govind Dave has come to the great Godman, Vallabhacharya. It is the year Savant 1558. Dave Ji came and asked with courteousness, "The Gita says, O man! You go to a good guru and bow before him – if you bow before a knowledable person, your sorrows will go away. Don't hide anything from your guru and God. You should tell the matters of your heart to only two people – one, to your guru, and the second, to God. Don't tell it to the world. It is the rule of the world to bring a fallen person further down. If you don't find a guru, tell it to God. See, there is no difference between love and devotion. Both mean the same thing. Narad Ji has even gone so far as to say –

"**Sa tasmin param prem rupa.**" In the second chapter, Narad Ji said what is devotion. Devotion is like great love. In devotion and love, whether it is the lover or the beloved, they always want to listen time and again from their beloved, "Yes, I love you." The Lord is all-knowing, but still he sometimes wants to hear this from the humans. Yes, you should not tell the Lord only your sorrows, but your happiness also. O Lord, we are extremely grateful to you that you have given us this body, you have given me this family, and you have given me wealth and property. And, don't ever ask God for anything.

The guru asked Govind Dave this question – "**Kutshchinta Bruvan?**" (Meaning, what is the worry?) He said, Guru ji, I have given everything to the Lord. Then? Then why are there lines of worry on your face? He said, "Maharaj, we are not God-like as you are. The worldly desires are very strong. These worldly problems and thoughts about afterlife still trouble us." The scriptures say – "**Sansar ghor patang kirane dahyati manavah.**" (Meaning, sufferings brought about by fate, sufferings brought about by worldly matters, and spiritual sufferings still trouble us.) "Although I have dedicated myself to the Lord, but when I sit down to serve him, my mind keeps wandering here and there. The worldly problems trouble me. My daughter has not got married till now. I don't have the capability to offer a 56-course meal to God, and I don't even have the wisdom. I don't know the art of impressing the Lord. Maharaj, there are not one, but many worries. It is as if there is a huge forest fire and I am trapped amidst it. Show me some path. O Lord, remove my worries. Enable my mind to concentrate in God's service. Enable me to derive pleasure out of God's service. Maharaj, sometimes

I worry about time, sometimes fate troubles me – "**Grih karaj nana janjala, te ati durgam sail visala.**" Emotions flood my heart. Sometimes, even this body does not support me, and I am not able to serve the Lord." Worry has been called a serpent. The great man who was sitting in the cremation ground told me what types of worries trouble human beings. He showed me the true picture of those worries. Celestial Gods also worry. From a mosquito to a celestial being, everyone worries.

The sages say that one falls ill due to worry. The high-charactered people are afraid of falling, those whose character is not high are also afraid of falling in society. "**Viten kulat bhayam.**" (Meaning, the merchant worries about money.) He has accumulated wealth with a lot of difficulties. His son shouldn't spend all his wealth in futile pursuits. As a person grows in age, his greed increases. In the childhood, greed is less. The child forgets the event of his childhood, an adult does not forget. There is a lot of greed. "**Viten kulat bhayam.**" When the soul does not offer the wealth earned from noble means to God, then that income will bring sorrow to your house. By giving charity, wealth becomes pure. Impure wealth is not offered to the Lord. God is pure forever. He will not accept impure wealth. Impure wealth is spent in bad things or for treatment of diseases. Manu Maharaj has said that human beings should always be divided into 10 parts. We have said in the beginning only, that there is an unbreakable relationship between God and human souls. Whatever you earn should also be divided into 10 parts. Knowledge should also be divided into 10 parts. Thoughts should also be divided into 10 parts. Otherwise, Bhrithari has said – "**Viten kulad bhayam manad bhayam.**" The person who has got prestige is afraid of ill-fame. "You can humiliate only the proud." One who is not proud, can not be humiliated. "**Bale ripu bhayam.**" (Meaning, the strong have the fear of the enemy.) There are many types of strengths – of beauty, of knowledge, of body, there are many types of strengths. So, the strong fear the enemy – "**In success, one meets fake friends and real enemies.**"

“**Rupam jara bhayam.**” (Meaning, the beautiful people fear old age.) There is no treatment for old age. “**Shastre vadi bhayam.**” (Meaning, the person who has knowledge fears discussion.) “**Gune khal bhayam.**” (Meaning, the person who has good qualities fears the evil people.) “**Kale vritantmay.**” (Meaning, everyone fears death.) Parikshit has said, “**Kale vyal mukh grass nirnash he tave.**” The human beings are afraid of the black serpent of death. If the snake swallows the person, then also he will die and if the snake spits poison out, then also the person will die from its poison. So, everyone is troubled by the fear of death. The nature of death is curvaceous like the serpent. No one has the wealth of time. We are all poor. So, the great men call out again and again, brother hurry up-

“**What you have to do tomorrow, do today, what you have to do today, do now, Within moments, calamity will strike, when will you do what you want to do??**”

Today, in society people think that when old age comes, we will take the name of the Lord. Taking the name of God is not some post-retirement job. Till then, it will become too late. Only fresh flowers are offered in worship. The stale flower of old age is not offered to God. Who knows about tomorrow? If death gives you one slap, then you will have to vacate this body that is your house. So, Mehta ji has said –

“**He ne maria madaria ye to maya matlab ki**
Bhai baat kare kal ki, khabar nahi pal ki re bhai...
Dhan jovan tero aave re jaave chaya badal ki
Khabar nahi pal ki re bhai baat kare kal ki...
Ram ne bhaji hari ne bhaj le kaune jaane kal ki...
Bhai baat kare kal ki re bhai baat kare kal ki...”

So, O Arjun! This serpent of death troubles the human soul. God is explaining to Arjun. Arjun, the kings that you are worrying about, don’t think that they did not exist before today or they will not exist after you. One who is born is certain to die. One who dies is certain to be born. “**Tasmat utisth yudhaya krit nischay.**”

The fear of death troubles those who are stuck in worldly

desires more. The more you get stuck in worldly desires, the more your desire to live increases. No one has the wealth of time. The intelligent person is one who forgets the past. The future is unknown. We only have to improve our present. The disciple who is sitting at the feet of the master is saying, "Maharaj, three types of worries have surrounded my mind." See, those people for whom you are worrying are not going to put a crown on your head. If one or two generations after your death, your photograph falls by mistake, then no one is going to replace the glass on that photograph even. Then, who are you worrying for? **"You are alone in this crowd. Before death, no one was yours. After death also there is going to be no one whom you can call yours."** Then, who are you worrying for?

People hold camps nowadays to remove worry and tensions. If worry could be treated so easily, then would Patanjali have written 'Yoga Darshan'. Neither would Vallabhacharya have written 'Navrattan Bodh'. If problems are solved without fasting, then why should anyone fast on 'ekadashi?' Today, people do the treatment, but they do not try to find the reason for the disease.

What is the place of worry? We see from our eyes. We hear from our ears. We feel from our skin. Where does all this go? To the mind. **"The place of worry is in the four constituents of the consciousness – 'man' (mind), 'budhi' (intellect), 'chitta' (will) and ahankaar' (ego)."** To do or not to do is in the mind, the mind questions. The brain takes the decision, and 'ego' does the work. These four things are the cause of worry. If I give 10 rupees in charity, the mind will analyse and think about it. The 'intellect' will ask a question that what was the benefit of giving that charity. The 'will' will think should I give 10 rupees or not? Then, the 'ego' will act and it will either make me give the 10 rupees or stop me from giving the 10 rupees. So, the family is not the reason for the worry. How should I behave with the family? That is the reason for worry. The daughter is not the reason for worry. The daughter has grown up, that is the reason for worry. How should I serve the Lord? That is the reason for worry. The Lord is not the reason for worry.

So, when Dave ji expressed his worries before the benevolent guru, then, the work of the guru is to remove doubts. "**The true guru is one who shows the path of truth.**" The good true does not tell his feelings, he tells the teachings of the scriptures. Because the whole world is something which has been seen by Vyas. All thoughts have come into Vyas' mind in some form or the other. The Mahabharata is the fifth Veda. So, the guru gives the proof of the Vedas. "**Where the scriptures end, from there the experiences of the guru start.**" "**Where the guru become silent, a vacuum comes over there and the soul reaches up to God.**"

Here, the acharya has written the epic "Navrattan Bodh" to remove the worries of the human beings, making Govind Dave a medium. Only the acharya knows this "Navrattan Bodh" completely. We have just made an attempt to understand it. Come, it is the order of the great men, it is the order of the scriptures, it is the tradition of the ancestors that your good deeds should be completed without any obstacle. For this, first of all, we have to remember the lord of 'riddhi-siddhi' (an epithet of Lord Ganesha), Ganpati Maharaj. See, we have 33 crore Gods and Goddesses in our mythology. If you don't have faith in any God, then bow before him thinking that he is a part of the Lord. Don't oppose anything or any person. By discarding opposition, the mind becomes peaceful. Come, let us pray so that we are granted the wisdom to understand the great epic of the acharya-

Gauri Ganesh Uma Ganesh Parvati Nandan Sriganesh
Sharnam Ganesh sharnam Ganesh Shankar Sriganesh
Gauri...
Vinayak Ganesh Vinayak Ganesh buddhidata Sriganesh
Sukh dayak Ganesh asht vinashak Ganesh. Gauri Ganesh...
Rishi Ganesh siddhi Ganesh vighanharta Sriganesh.
Gauri...
Gauri Ganesh Gauri Ganesh Parvati nandan Sriganesh.

The true guru is merciful. The feeling in the mind of the true guru is only that his disciple should benefit in all possible ways. The goal of the true guru is that at any time, in any way, he should lift up the disciple and make him reach the feet of the Lord. The guru becomes happy on seeing the curiosity of the disciple. If there is no Arjun, then whom will Krishna tell the Gita to? A devoted disciple has expressed his worry to the guru, so the Navrattan epic has come into being. 'Navrattan' deals with not only the worry of the mind, but also of the body. The reason for worry can be a disease of the body also. The lack of money can also be a reason for worry. So, the scriptures have suggested three things to remove this type of worry – mantras, jewels, and medicine. Your worry can be removed by mantras. The jewel should be like 'chintamani' (a jewel which is supposed to remove all worry), lapis-lazuli jewel, or like the 'sayamantak' (name of a jewel). All these jewels remove worry. Medicine also removes worry according to Ayurveda.

"**The teaching of a true guru is also like medicine, it is like a curing jewel, it is like a mantra.**" So, the true guru is one who does not do magic. Like the doctor tells the medicine, but the sick man has to eat the medicine himself. The doctor does not eat it. Here, Vallabhacharya also has the same feeling. O human souls, come, I will free you from this disease of emotions. This is the first couplet. We are beginning the journey. Here, the Navrattan has been created to free us from worry. The meaning of 'ratan' is light. So, the light can be in the form of a jewel also. Here, we will discuss jewels of nine types. Worry does not come through the pain giving planets. The nine planets and Rahu, Ketu etc. are not the reason for your worry. Rahu-Ketu don't have the time to trouble you.

"**Your thoughts, your intentions, your shortcomings are the evil planets that trouble you.**" Your thoughts, your desires are the reasons for your sorrow. Why didn't this work happen according to my wishes? I have to propitiate these nine planets. See, our Prahlad ji Maharaj has created 'Navdha Bhakti' (Nine

Types of Devotion) to remove all types of sorrow. 'Navdha Bhakti' has been created to remove all these nine types of sorrows. Even if one of these nine types of devotions come into us, then we believe that all types of anger, disease, and pain will be removed. Because it is said in the Upanishads –

"**Man eva manushyanam karanev bandh mokshyo.**" (Meaning, the mind is everything. If the mind is in adverse situation, then you will become sad. If the mind is in a situation which is according to its desires, then you will become happy.) So, the mind is the reason for happiness and sadness. God has said in the Gita – O Arjun –

"**Atamev ripu atamev bandhu.**" (Meaning, the soul is the friend of the soul. The soul is the enemy of the soul.) What is your behaviour like? Tell me!! 'Navdha Bhakti' says –

Prahlad says-

"Shravanam kirtanam vishno smaranam paad sevanam
Archanam vandanam dasyam sakhyam atma nivedanam."

These are the nine types of worship. What type of worship needs to be attached to each couplet, we will analyse this. These are nine jewels, these are nine planets, these are nine medicines, and these are nine types of devotion.

What can we say about Vallabhacharya here? He is a man of God, that is why he has said-

"**Krishna eva gatirmam, Krishna eva gatirmam,**
Krishna eva gatirmam."

The great man is saying that he is not worrying. I think about Him, so he worries about me. Arjun said – What are you saying? He said – Yes, if you think about me, then I will worry about you. If you want I will write it on a paper and sign it, or put my thumb impression on it, said the Lord. Listen Arjun-

"**Ananyashchintyanto ma ye janah paryupasate**
Tesha nityaniyuktanam yogekshem vahamyaham."

–Gita para 9, couplet 22

The 'gopis' said that God's language was not so simple. This is a misleading couplet. He says something and does something else. Arjun said, "Then O Lord, you will do everything for me." Lord said, "Yes, But only when you worship me with devotion –

Ananyashchintyanto ma ye jana...

Meaning, if you worship me with true devotion, are not separate from me for even one moment. It should not be like this that you worship me for only one hour in the morning and then forget about me-

"**Bhavo hi vidhate devta.**"

God has said this. One who worships me with true devotion, like the uninterrupted flow of a stream of oil, one who doesn't remove his mind from me for even one second. Our thoughts keep breaking. Sometimes we have affection for money, sometimes wife, sometimes prestige, sometimes our son. See, the Lord is not saying that you don't look after your family. You have to do that also. But, your mind should remain at the feet of Govind. Your family is thirsty for your body and wealth. "**God is thirsty for your love, not your worship.**" So, it has been said in 'Navrattan'. This is the worry of Govind Dave ji. How should I worship God? I don't have the capacity to offer a 56-course meal to God. I only have the water of the Yamuna and the basil leaves to offer God. "How should I worship you God?" God said, "I don't want your 56-course meal.

"**Patram pushpam phalam toyam**
yo me bhaktya prayachati...."

Meaning, whatever you give me, your love, flowers, fruits or water with 'love', I will accept that.

In "**Do Sau Vavan Vaishnavo**" there was a Padyanam Das ji who was not rich. He didn't have any property. So what? God is hungry for the feeling. What you are giving is not important. With what emotion you are giving is important. So, O God, we don't even know Sanskrit. I can't even say a couplet properly. Then, how should I attract you, God? From morning till night, I make not one but many mistakes. Then, how should I make you happy, God? This is my worry –

Shri ji baba din dyala bhakto tamaro jaan jo,
Hari gun gaata dosh pade tu seva hamari maan jo.

Tu apna di kai ne samajhiyon naam Tamara pran de
Daas upar daya karo to ho mahara kalyan hai.
Shri ji baba…
Din bandhu o dindayalu prarthna karun khadi-khadi
Go lok vaasi vaikunth vaasi buddhi hamari sudhar jo
Janam maran na bandhan chute aisi bhakti mane aap jo.
Shri ji baba…
Ant samay prabhu daya karije darshan deva aav jo
Daas upar daya kari nai charan kamal ma rakh jo.
Shri ji baba…

Govind ji's main question is regarding worry and how to be free oneself from worry. When he expressed this feeling, then the acharya started with the word 'worry' itself.

"Chinta na kaapi karya niveditatamarmah kadapiti!"

Meaning, to control its mind when the human soul emerges above thoughts and alternatives, then at that time worry is finished. If the person is doing 'ashtang yoga' then, then he experiences 'samadhi' (true bliss). If the person is in the devotional level, then he enters the world of God, i.e. he sees God. Pay attention that this field of thought is of 'shuddhadvait." In 'addvaitism' two points meet. '**Aham brahamasmi**' happens. A person goes from 'me' to 'you'. In 'shuddhadvait' this does not happen. We are sitting here. God should talk to us. Our material aspect or the human soul wants to retain its identity. It does not disappear. When a drop falls from a cloud, then from the time it falls from the cloud, till the time it reaches the earth, it has its own identity. As soon as it touches the ocean, it loses its identity. During the time it fell from the cloud, to the time it reached the ocean, it had its separate identity. Afterwards, it became one element. This is the ideology of 'advaitvaad'. Here, this is not so.

When the worrying nature of the human soul is stopped, then the state of mind of the yogis which is also called '**nirvikalp samadhi**' (state of bliss) is achieved. For us, the meaning of that is that God and his work can be seen. That we get to be close to God. Meaning we get '**saamipya mukti**' (freedom due to closeness). Maharaj, if I myself become Krishna, then what enjoyment will I get from amorous activities. When Parikshit asked this question, that God is himself the protector of righteousness, then how did God indulge in amorous activities with the gopis? This is an inappropriate thing to do. Then, Shukdev ji said – "There is no difference between gopis and Krishna. The one who is gopi is Krishna. The one who is Krishna is gopi. Whatever the gopi eats, drinks, sees, and hears is Krishna and only Krishna.

One gopi was sitting at the banks of river Yamuna. Narad ji came and asked her – Gopi, what is the matter? Gopi said – Maharaj, I have got a disease. He has gone, but he has given me this disease. I have been struck by this disease, Maharaj. What does he know about love? I am crying for him. Narad ji said, "Gopi, you are lying. There are no tears in your eyes. Gopi said, "Maharaj, you may have written the 'Bhakti Sutra,' but you have forgotten something. Even though you may be the guru of devotion, you have forgotten something-

"**Pritam chavi nainan basi ab par chavi kahan samaaye**
Bhari saray rahim lakhi pathik aap chali jaaye"

Meaning, Krishna resides in these eyes, then how will tears stay in these eyes. So, even though you may have written the Bhakti Sutra, to learn true devotion and true love, you will have to come to us because-

Yehi ras ne jane che brij keri gopi,
Yehi ras ne jane che shukdev jogi,
Kai kai jane che nar saya bhogi.

So, '**chinta kayati**' meaning don't worry even a little bit. One who has offered everything in his life to God, why should he worry? Then, Dave ji folded his hands and asked – So, Guru ji, is there anything lacking in my prayers. Have I done something deceitful? Some people try to deceive God also. Then that person will certainly do deceit with his family and the society.

So, Dave ji, have you really surrendered everything? We pray to God from morning till night. We also bend our bodies and pray to him. But, our heart does not bow to him. We are not able to put aside our ego. I have 20 lakh rupees. Till this feeling is in your mind, till then worry is there.

Nahin koi as janma jag mahi prabhuta pai jahi mad nahi.

When the story of Indradev came up, then God said that O king, the one on whom I bestow my blessings, I take away position, money, and status from him. Indra said, "Why so? Maharaj?" God said, "O husband of Shachi! The devotee becomes proud due to these three things. I never let my devotees feel proud. Like a cow licks away the dirt on her calf because she knows that this dirt is mine; similarly, if any dirt sticks to my devotee, then I clean that dirt. God cleans the dirt of pride that sticks to a devotee. God himself looks after the human soul as a mother. As a mother does not give a knife into the hand of a child until the child is old enough to understand how to use it, similarly, till the devotee becomes mature, God keeps him away from wealth. Keep calm, you will definitely get what is in your fate. It can be delayed, but no injustice will be done to you.

Dave ji says that he has surrendered himself before God by "**Kayen vacha man**" (body, speech, and mind) in every way, he has surrendered before God. But, has he surrendered in reality. See, we donate money in the donation box, but do we ever have the courage to donate our good deeds. Human beings indulge in deceit. But, the deceit does not work in front of God. If still there are some desires remaining in you, then tell God that I still feel like eating gulab-jamun (sweetmeat). You need to have complete surrender.

Ab saunp diya is jivan ka sab bhar
tumhare charanon mein
Hai jeet tumhare charnon mein,
prabhu haar tumhare charnon mein.

(Meaning, I have put all the burdens of my life in your feet. Now, my defeat is in your feet and my victory is in your feet.)

Have you really surrendered everything? Till you have not surrendered your intelligence, you will worry. The little infant who drinks his mother's milk is completely dependant on his mother, so he is carefree. He doesn't have any ego. So, the mother does every little thing for the child. Once the child learns how to do things himself, then the mother does not look after him. She says that I have kept food for you, if you want to eat it, you can, otherwise it is your wish. Yes, till he was innocent, she used to look after him fully. So, surrender your intelligence completely before God. If human beings doubt, they ask, "Why this? Then, why this?" God has said in Gita "**Arjun natr sanshay** (don't doubt)." In society, usually people follow each other. If one person has kept an ekadashi fast, then another person will also keep the fast. Why do you copy another person? If your heart thinks today to be ekadashi, then you observe ekadashi fast today. Why do you wait until tomorrow? If you wait for tomorrow, your entire life will get over.

"**Bhakti ke liye anukulta ki pratiksha mat karo**"

(Don't wait for good times to come before you start your devotion to God.)

Like the waves of the ocean are never silent, similarly the conflicts of life are never silent.

The person who has offered himself to God, he has become free of worry. Human beings function on faith. We don't maintain relationships with someone on whom we don't have faith. Possibly, you have not reposed full faith in God till now-

"**Lokvattu, lila kevalyam.**" God lifted Goverdhan on his finger for seven days, for what? Only to tell the human soul that see my strength. God is telling Arjun – Arjun, if you come to me even after sinning, I will free you from your sins. This does not mean that you are free to sin. "**The meaning of this is only that "If you surrender completely, then I am with you.**" What did Gajendra have? The crocodile had dragged him away. His family had left him. At that time, what did Gajendra have? He only had a lotus flower to offer God. Lotus meaning his heart. He offered that to God, and he was saved. Offer your innermost self to God and say that Maharaj, I am standing before you. If small things trouble you, this means that you have not surrendered completely. If you surrender completely, then think that whatever is happening in my life is happening due to the will of God. Then, why worry? But, we do not do this. That is why Arjun asked the question –"**Stith pragya ka bhasha?**" (Meaning, how does a devoted and balanced person behave?) God said that one who does not worry, who does not have any greed, one who is satisfied in mind and body, one who is not disturbed by profit or loss and victory or defeat, one who is of stable mind, one who is 'aniket'. 'Aniket' does not mean someone who does not have a house, 'aniket' means someone who is not obsessed with his house and material desires. If this were not so, then the name of Janak would not have come in the Gita. Janak stays in a palace, but, the palace does not stay in Janak.

"The meaning of surrendering yourself to God is to have full faith in God. Does God not worry about you? God is your father. "**Aham bij prad pita**" (I am your father). So, is there any father who does not worry about his son? However old the son might be, the parents worry about him. It is the nature of the mother to worry about the son. She will definitely worry, so:

"**Matsamah paatki nasti papaghni twatasama na hi**
Avem gyatva mahadevi yatha yogyam tatha kuru"

God, just like the greedy man loves wealth, the lusty man loves women, similarly I love sin. There is no bigger sinner than me. It is a very beautiful feeling. You serve God, you don't love God. The 'gopi' loves God. The 'gopi' sometimes cries, then sometimes she gives a betel leaf. The 'gopi' doesn't only pray. There are no rules in love. Talk to God. Today, I am feeling warm. Maharaj, are you thirsty, should I give you water? Should I make tea for you? You will say, God does not drink tea, He drinks milk. He can drink tea also. You try to offer him lovingly. **God is thirsty not for your service, but for your love.**

"Akhil dehinaantaratmadrak, vikhan sarthito vishwa guptaye."

Many great men say that whatever you receive, first of all, offer it to God. Become one with God. God does not want your body. We have heard that there is a garland of human skulls in God Mahadev's neck. What is the meaning of this? Whose skull is this? He wants Yagnavalkya's skull, he wants Shukdev's skull. He wants Vasishth's skull. Only one who has the courage can give this. Only one who has devotion can worship. Meera had done true worship. This is a work of great bravery. It is not the work of cowards. Like Kabir

"**Yeh to ghar hai prem ka khala ka ghar nahin**
Sees utare hathi kare so paide ghar mahin."

You have to offer everything here. If you are not able to do this, consider yourself a servant of God. Think that God has given this body to me for 100 years to serve him. This body and this wealth, I am not the owner of this, but the caretaker. When my time finishes, I will have to give everything back to him. As your sense of ownership decreases, your worries will decrease. You will feel peaceful. Otherwise, however much you close your nostrils and do yoga, it will all be useless. It is said in the Mahabharata – "When greed increases, sin increases. When sin increases, temperature will increase, worries will increase, struggle will increase." So, accumulate less. Limit your necessities. God has given all these things to serve him. He is the owner of all these. This body is also not mine. Whenever God wishes, he will ask me to vacate this body, which is like a house taken on rent. If your thoughts are such then – "**Chinta na karya**"–you should not worry at any time.

The goal of saying and listening to this discourse is also to free oneself from worry, to achieve bliss, to have faith in God. 'Ka' means God and 'tha' means stability. By listening to 'katha' (discourse) your faith in God becomes strong because in a discourse, the nature and influence of God is described. You listen to a discourse with faith, with curiosity. In a discourse, the curiosity should not be to evaluate the holy man speaking the discourse. Logic and reasoning should be done with politeness. Don't ever indulge in warped logic. A reasoning mind often deviates into irrationality. If you listen to a discourse with devotion, then you become one with God. Some people read newspapers and magazines a lot. The shortcomings of the writer come into the books. So, you should read only those books whose writer has realised God. Read Shrimadbhagwad, read the Gita, read the Upanishads, read the Ramayana. What can be said about Ved Vyas? He is the artistic manifestation of God. Read the Gita. Every alphabet of the Gita is filled with intelligence. In other books, the shortcomings of the writer come into the books. If once your mind becomes warped, then it will take a long time to set it right. Be careful that no dark spot comes in your mind and brain. So, it is said-**Asango tu asang ho ja**. (meaning bad company, you go away from me). The meaning of being away from bad company is not that you should not stay in a family or that you should not go to the market. No, stay in a family, go to the market, but your mind should always be in the lotus feet of Shri Krishna. Like the 'gopis' live-

Vikretu kamakhil gop kanya murari paadarpit chitvriti
Dadhyadikam moh vashad vochad
Govind Damodar Madhaveti.

The 'gopis' do every work, but their mind is immersed in the feet of Shri Krishna. Like Sita is in the Ashoka garden in her body, but her mind is somewhere else-

"**Nij pad nayan diye man ram pad kamal leen**"

When Hanuman saw mother Janki, then the mother's eyes were on her feet and her mind was in Ram's feet. It is said in the Gita – no one can escape what is destined for him. No one can be free from the duties of the body. Duties of the body means hunger, thirst, sleep etc.

Even after obtaining knowledge about the supreme element, there can be no escape from the duties of the body and destiny. The word 'Bhagwan' has arisen from the mineral 'bhag'. One which has six 'bhags' is God. The Vedas say–God is one whose body is not made of blood, bone, and flesh. That form of you which is true, blissful, and peaceful; that is God.

The acharya is hinting here. The scholars of the

Shrimadbhagwat have said clearly "**Krishnastu bhagwan swayam** (Krishna is God incarnate)." There can be no argument and counter-argument on this. Krishna is the merciful, pitiful God himself.

O human soul! When you have surrendered everything to him, when you have dedicated yourself to him, then he will look after your welfare. Now, let him worry, why do you worry. The Bhagwat says that this nature of God serves you 24 hours. This wind never takes a vacation. The Sun never rises late. The earth has never refused to give food. Have the clouds ever refused to rain? God worries about you 24 hours. So, "**chinta na kaapi karya...**" There is no such mother in the world who does not worry about her children, no matter how the children may be.

"**Kuputro jayate kwachit pitu mata na bhavati**"

God says I am one who cleanses the sinners, but you don't become a sinner. You say that I have never sinned, my neighbour has made this mistake. If you appear like Ahilya, then God will himself come to deliver you. If you say "God I am fallen, I am poor," then God will come himself to help you. God knows everything about the situation a human being is in or the thoughts that a human being is thinking.

"**Janat preet reet raghurai.**"

Shandilya Maharaj has said that He is the one to give limitless fruits, then why do you worry? **Kadapi chinta na karya** (never worry). Then what should we do? Maharaj said, Dave ji, you do only one work, think about Him."

"**Tasmat sarveshu kaleshu mamanusmar.**" Meaning, O human being, if you will think about me, I will worry about you.

This first couplet is the first jewel of 'Navrattan Bodh.' Like there are nine planets, this first couplet is the Sun of this book. The Sun stays in one sun-sign for 15 days. This first couplet is the Sun. The Sun is a form of Lord Krishna. Those 15 days meaning the bright half of the lunar month + the dark half of the lunar month. Krishna resides in these. He will protect you always.

In 'Navdha Bhakti' this first couplet is '**sakhya bhakti**' (sakhya means friendship, bhakti means devotion). In 'sakhya bhakti,' God is called the nourisher. He is called the merciful, loving God. Love exists only among equals. God is like the friend of the devotee. Here, giving the example of Arjun, Vallabhacharya is saying that you don't worry. Your relationship with God is from time immemorial, like Brahma and Saraswati, like wave and ocean, like heat and temperature, like mountains and their coolness. No one can separate the Sun from its rays. Similarly, O human being! You are a part of God. God is very soon going to shower his blessings on you. Why are you wandering here and there? You only stop worrying, just remember – **Shri Krishna sharnam mam, Shri Krishna sharnam mam, Shri Krishna sharnam mam.**

Glory be to Dwarkadheesh (King of Dwarka), Glory be to Krishna.

✻ CHAPTER 2 ✻

"Nivedanam tu smartvyam sarvatha tadwashe janeh
Sarveshvarasch sarvatama nijechaatah karishyati."

–*Second couplet*

Without the blessings of God, this mortal world, which is nothing but a manifestation of God's sense of humour, seems to be real. Due to the magic spell cast by God, this world seems to be real. When the king of Brij, the great lover, the beloved of the 'gopis' showers his blessings on humankind, then first of all the devotee offers his heart, mind, nature, ego, and the senses to which he has been a slave at the feet of God. He starts serving the world with the feeling in his heart that this world is a creation of God and whatever he has got is a blessing of God. At the time of serving, there should be only one feeling in the mind of the devotee – "**Nath tavaasmi.**" "**Krishna tavaasmi.**" O God, whatever I may, however I may be; I am yours. If God does not shower his blessings on humankind, then the Bhagwati Shruti, Upanishads and the main Gods, holy men, and sages depicted in the epics lose their meaning.

When the human soul surrenders everything before God, then God is eager to help the human soul and to deliver him from difficulties. Our scriptures say-

"**Bhaktianveshdon tatparo prativrato bhakti pradoto hito**"

Tatparo – means 'eager'. He is ever eager to help you. In the Gita, he himself says – "**Yoga kshem vahaamyaham.**" (I am eager to do your welfare.)

In the beginning of the second couplet, the word has come '**nivedan (**dedication).' When the word 'nivedan (dedication)' is taken in its ordinary context, when the meaning of the word as it is used in day-to-day language is taken, it means to form a relationship with God. When the disciple takes the traditional eight-lettered 'mantra' from the guru at the time of initiation, when he accepts the gift of this mantra, then it becomes certain that he will get a place in the lotus feet of God. The whole process takes only a moment. But, to carry out this process, to emerge true to this process, takes an entire lifetime. The meaning of 'to dedicate' is not to dedicate outside elements, but to dedicate the innermost elements. I dedicate my five senses, my brain, my heart, my life, everything to God. If this does not happen and your senses are attracted somewhere else, then you will fail in your goal. The success of the five senses is only in that they remain engaged in remembering God, in serving God. Some people took the vow in front of their gurus to serve God, and wore the traditional string of beads in their neck, but did not surrender completely. But, God himself makes arrangements that the person who has surrendered before me, even though half-heartedly, one day he will surrender fully before me and will attain the goal of his life.

In the Shrimadbhagwat, God Shukdev introduced two such souls to Parikshit. These people had not dedicated their inner self completely to God, so they had to be born as trees. God is merciful, God is kind. He loves his devotees. He had pity on them and freed them from their form as trees. At the time of being freed, Yamlarjun said these words:

"**Vani gunanukathane shravano kathayam**
Hasto ch karmsu manstavah padyornah."

"O God! Now our voice will always sing your praises. May our ears always hear your discourse. May our hands always do your work, and may our heart always be in your lotus feet." God, our senses had been attracted towards material desires. That is why we failed. O God! Now have pity on us and make our senses follow you. When the senses go towards worldly desires, then these desires make the human being mad. In the scriptures, this is the definition that has been given of lust.

"Lust is that to fulfil which the human being becomes blind, he becomes deaf, he loses all his logic and reasoning abilities."

When Surdas was stricken with lust, he sat on a corpse and crossed the river. He could not even hear the noise of the heavy storm that was raging. Lightning was flashing. He thought a snake to be a rope and climbed upstairs using that. So, till the senses are attracted towards the worldly desires, till then a desire to indulge in worldly desires will arise in you. "**The action that you take to fulfil your lust is not pure, and this impure deed will become your fate in the future and the soul will not get deliverance.**"

In the scriptures, the place of '**mumukshatv**' (salvation, moksha) has been called very difficult to achieve. The first difficult thing to achieve is the human body, the second difficult place to achieve is salvation, and according to 'Vivek Churamani' to see a true saint is the most difficult thing of all.

If anything in this world seems attractive to you, then outwardly whatever you may be doing, from your inside you are asleep. You are attracted towards a poisonous substance. Without the blessings of the guru, without the blessings of God, the human soul cannot rise upwards. Pay attention – "**By doing a good deed, human beings become free. By doing a bad deed, human beings become slaves.**"

Doing a good deed, to take a round around the mountain ('parikrama'), to offer a 56-course feast to God, all these are done by money. You should try to take a vow that I will not lie from tomorrow. But, you will not be able to do this. As Goswami ji has said, this is only possible when the blessings of God are with you –

Ati hari kripa jaahi par hoin, pave deh yeh marag soi
Binu satsang vivek na hohi, ram kripa binu sulabh na soi

Conquering your senses enables you to get closer to God.

There is a worry in the mind of Govind Dave ji. "**Worry and**

funeral pyre both burn the human body." A funeral pyre burns the human body in a very short time, but worry burns the body every second. Is the birth of human beings only for struggle, tension, and suffering? In the journey of life, on the right hand side is the ditch and on the left hand side is the deep well. God has had mercy on us and has sent great men to this earth. He has not changed the world, but he has changed the outlook of human beings. He has made the life, which was like poison, like the nectar of immortality. In life, there are stones and pebbles in our path, there will be troubles in our path, people of society will talk against us, our body will not cooperate with us, our mind will indulge in reasoning, but the great men have taught us that those people who have a habit of looking at flowers, look at flowers only and those people who have a habit of looking at thorns, look at thorns only. You don't look at the thorns. Ravan is here, Duryodhan is here, Hiranyakashipu is here. If you want to remove them, become Prahlad, become Krishna, become gopi. Pay attention-

"**Jagat ka dayitv jeev ka nahin jagdish ka hai.**"

(Meaning, the responsibility of the world is on God's shoulders, not on the shoulders of the human being.)

"**Jad chetan gun doshmay vishv kinh kartar.**" (God has made the world as it is – full of good and bad qualities.)

This world is full of good and bad things. This is due to God's will. We have to see the good things not the bad things.

Dave ji saluted acharya ji. Acharya ji saw the lines of worry on Dave ji's face, so Vallabhacharya said, "There should be no lines of worry on the face of people who have dedicated themselves to God. Why are you worried?"

The first couplet is like jasper. The first devotion is 'sakhya bhakti' (friendly devotion). In 'Navdha Bhakti' the first type of devotion has been told as 'sakhya bhakti' because the human soul has worry and God is worried about the human soul.

"In the Upanishads, there is a story of two parrots. One parrot used to fly from one branch to another. If he got a bitter fruit, he used to shout and if he got a sweet fruit, he used to laugh. The second parrot is just watching the first parrot, he does not say anything, he is detached. The first parrot told the second parrot that he was going to another tree because there were no sweet fruits on this tree. The second parrot said to him that he would give him some words and whenever he remembered him he should call him and the second parrot would come and meet him because they were both friends. How beautifully the sages have described the soul and God. The parrot who ate the sweet and sour fruits is the soul and the detached parrot is God who is waiting patiently. God is saying to the soul that I am waiting for you. This tree of sweet and bitter fruits is nothing else but one birth or another birth. When the soul in the form of the parrot came to a tree, it forgot the sign that God had given it. So, he was not able to see God. That sign is nothing else but the mantra that God gave it by which the parrot could see God. The soul accepted that it had forgotten the signal words that God had given it. The sages say –

"Na mantra na yantra tadapi ch na jaane stutimaho
Na chvahanam dhyanam tadapi ch na jaane stuti kathah."

(Devi apradh kshama strotra)

Na jane mudraste tadapi ch na jaane vilpanam
Param jaane maatstavadnusarnam klesh harnam.

(Devi apradh kshama strotra)

So, O mother, I have forgotten that mantra. Here, this is the reason for the worry on Dave ji's face. God does not forget humans, human beings forget God. This is the only reason for worry. So, acharya ji asked him – "Why are you worried?"

What should I say, Maharaj? My daughter has not got married till now. Then, I worry about feeding and looking after my family. I am not able to offer a 56-course meal to God also. This is also a matter for worry. I had taken a vow that everything that belonged to me I would offer to God. But still, I use this wealth for myself. Is this all right? This is also a worry. God, how should I make you happy? I don't know any mantras. I am absolutely foolish. I am worried about this also.

See, the work of a true guru is to give you knowledge, to give you realisation, to destroy bad thoughts. The sages have described this as the meaning of education in the scriptures.

"**Shikshate kshalyate anyen sah iti shikhsa.**"

Meaning, the process through which impurities are taken away, and, purities are implanted.

True knowledge is that which destroys lust, which destroys the bad thoughts of the disciple. Otherwise, anyone can teach how to add two and two. "**That knowledge which is not able to destroy lust, that is useless.**"

The one who gives knowledge is the guru. According to the 'Amarkosh', the definition of a disciple is – "**One who can be ruled is a disciple.**" The disciple never disobeys orders. He never argues. If the guru has told him to go and clean the cowshed, then he will do it.

One such incident occurred in the life of Nanak Dev ji. Nanak Dev told his son to go and clean the cowshed. His son went, but he did not clean the cowshed. He thought that tomorrow he would sit on the seat of the Guru after his father's death, then how could he clean the cow shed. Then, Nanak Dev told him-

"One who cannot clean the cowshed, how will he cleanse the bad habits of my disciples. Son, you are not able enough to sit on the seat of the Guru." Nanak Dev did not give his seat to his son. He gave his seat to his disciple, Angad Dev. What tradition are you talking about, Maharaj? Tradition applies to the throne, tradition applies to your father's property. There is no tradition for God. Dronacharya had not given his son, Ashwathama complete knowledge. Was he not capable of giving full knowledge to his son? Why did he not give – "**Vidya vinyen shobhate.**" Meaning, knowledge is given only to the humble person. Knowledge is not to put someone down or to show someone as lowly, but knowledge is to recognize one's own self. Who am I? Who am I? Recognize yourself.

So, acharya ji is a guru of the whole world. He is giving knowledge here. Then, why are you worrying, O human being?

In the second couplct is shown what a human being has to do. What is God like? What does God want in return? See, the human soul and God both have a partnership. Don't consider both of them as separate. Whatever good qualities and habits God has, a human soul also has those qualities and habits. The only difference is that he knows and you don't know. Human beings have complete powers to become God. In the 'Valmiki Ramayan', Ram did not say at any place that he was God. Everywhere, he gave his introduction as – "I am Dashrath's son." He only said this. Nowhere did he exhibit his power because he wanted to tell the world that everyone had the power to become God.

"**As prabhu hriday achat avichari, sakal jeev jag deen dukhari.**" In the second couplet, two incidents are happening. What does the human soul have to do? What does God do? Even after surrendering everything to God, the human soul should not become inactive. Pay attention –

"In the yoga method, the path by which we accomplish something, after attaining that thing, that path is discarded. The asanas, pranayam, restraint, meditation, as these progress, the previous stages are discarded. But, in the path of devotion, the path through which you get fulfilment, even after obtaining fulfilment, that path is not discarded. Shukdev ji said to Parikshit - Rajan, the son of Nand had reached the house of Nand. Yashoda had realised this, so God cast a magic spell on Yashoda due to which she forgot that this was God incarnate. So, here Nand and Yashoda have got God, but still Yashoda and Nand did not discard their prayers. They did not stop keeping fasts and offering prayers. Even if you are able to see God, then also the human soul should not leave the path of prayer of God. There is no surety of this world. The only way of being released from the whirlpool of worldly desires is to take shelter under God's arms. The 'yogis' depend on their yoga, whereas the devotees depend on the power of God.

While speaking the second couplet, on seeing the lines of worry on Govind Dave ji's face, acharya ji said–

"Nivedanam tu smaratavyam tadrishejaneh
Sarveshvarashch sarvatama nijechhatah karishyati." –2

When a human being has surrendered himself to God, then why worry? This means that either he has not surrendered completely, there is still some faith reposed in the money or the offspring. Narad ji once asked God, "God, how do you keep your devotees?" God said, "There is only way to do that, Narad." "What, O Lord?"

"**Jimi balak raakhen mahtari.**" Meaning, like a mother keeps her innocent child, I also keep my disciples like that. If the child does not have enough sense to realise what to do, then the mother knows what to do, what does the child want or not want.

"**Naraddhitasi vidhina vivedhopchareh kirunksh chintan pare na kritam vachomi.**"

(Devi apradh kshama strot)

Meaning, Mother, customs and traditions and formalities, I don't know anything. God said what do you know? God, I don't know anything. My thoughts are also very bad. God, good thoughts also don't come into my mind, only bad thoughts come. Even while going for the religious discourse, this thought comes into my mind that I am going for the religious discourse for three hours, have I locked the house properly or not? Some thief may come while I am away. Do you want that a theft should take place at your house? See, don't ever think about something which you don't want to happen. Human beings have formed a habit of thinking bad thoughts. Leave alone doing good deeds, they cannot even think good thoughts today. Keep in mind –

"**The thought is the mother of the deed.**"

As you think, so shall you do, because before doing a deed, the idea originates in your mind. Should I pluck flowers for worship or not? So, first the thought will come in your mind and then you will do the deed. If the thought is not pure, then how will the deed be pure? So, the human being is accepting that O Mother, my thoughts were impure – "**Ruksh chintan pare na kritam vachomi.**" Meaning, God, how can my deeds be pure when my thoughts are not pure.

The meaning of a person who has dedicated himself is that a devotee does not have doubts. "I will do this deed." In the Gita, God has forbidden to think about the future. The reason for this was that in thinking about the future, the desire for the fruits of labour grows, due to which even the deed becomes impure. So, Yogeshwar has said – Where my God keeps me, however he keeps me, till when he keeps me, is acceptable to me.

"Mahara natraja thara nachaya nachun re.
Jo tu thokar maar girave lakdi jyun gir jaoon,
Jo tu maathe pe bithave to bhi na sharmaaoon re.
Mahara girdhar lal thara nachaya nachoon re,
Thare ghar mein rahoon nirantar thari haat sajaoon re
Thaare ghan thaare jan ki seva tahal bajaaoon re
Mahara girdhar lal.......
Jis rang la kapda pahiraave vaiso hi bhesh banaaoon
Jaise bol bulave much se vaisi baat sunaaoon re
Mahara girdhar lal......
Mahara natwar lal......"

There was Tukaram ji Maharaj in your Maharashtra whose life was like this. See, the devotee does not belong to any community. The saint can take birth anywhere. The saint does not belong to any one person. He belongs to the world. Does the Shankaracharya belong only to the Hindus? Vallabhacharya belongs to everyone. He is a bridge, which takes human beings to Gods. Whoever wants can make him a medium to reach God.

Bhakt beej palte nahin jug jaahi anant
Oonch neech kul jag kahe akhir sant hai sant.
Tukaram ji kahe-
Dehachiti chori bhakti chaach deva,
Udhad daad deva data udhad daad deva.

So, when you have dedicated everything to God, then this means that whatever is here, everything is given by God, you have to keep this feeling. Shukdev has said – O human, half of your life is spent in feeding and looking after your family, "**udaram-bharino jeeva...**

See, we are not blaming anyone here. We are only telling you that the lives of the worldly human beings have become like this. Otherwise, you should understand one thing that if you leave the worldly path and immediately join the path of devotion, God will not accept you immediately. God is not saying this. Here, you do not have to leave everything and go after God. But, instead, you have to keep God in the middle of every work. Whatever deed you do, keep God in the middle and do it. Then, every deed will turn into devotion. Arjun had asked – What does a dedicated person eat? Then, God had said, "See, he also eats like normal human beings. He also does daily rituals like normal human beings. But, he is aware that these deeds are not done by me, but by my senses." So, in every act, keep this feeling that I am not doing this for myself, but for God." **If I am bathing, then I am not bathing myself, but I am bathing God. When I am walking, I am taking a circle around God. When I am sleeping, I am meditating on God. Even while I am sleeping, I am thinking about God. I am not sleeping!** Then, the question arises that what is the benefit of doing all this. When I have to do business and earn money, then I should do business. Why should I think all this? This is so because by keeping God in the middle, you will shirk from lies and deceits. See, you cannot deceive God. He knows everything. But, today, human beings try to deceive God also. In the materials used for worshipping God, they indulge in deceit. One who deceives God, will he shirk from deceiving the society? Remember, deceit is only there, where there is a feeling of non-belonging, and God belongs to you. God is my own, Govind is mine, Gopal is mine. Shri Banke Bihari, Nandlal is mine (all epithets of Lord Krishna).

"I am yours,"–say this to God. Whatever deed the human beings do after keeping God in the middle, that is an act of dedicating oneself to God. "**Keeping God with you all the time is forming a true relation with God.**" In my mind, in every deed of mine, God remains with me, this is the true relation with God. In my speech, in my sight, in my breath, in my heart beats, God should be with me – this is the true relation with God. What will happen due to this? What event will take place in this situation? What should we say, Maharaj?

Just now, someone was saying to me that the detail with which you speak, we have not heard elsewhere. What can I say to you? Why am I doing all this? Whose orders am I acting upon? What will be the result of this? This is the age of science. I know that what I am speaking is being heard by 20 crore people due to the modern means of telecommunication. What will the result of this be? What effect will this have on the society? I am aware of this, the responsibility for this also rests on my shoulders. On every word I speak, either people will repose their faith or they will reject my thoughts.

My work is not to break and join. My work is to only bring the facts forward. What is unclean, I have to clean that. What proof has Lord Shri Krishna given in the Geeta? See, you will never find anything like this elsewhere. He has said –

"There are some people whose knowledge has been covered with ash. There are some people on whose knowledge dust has spread, like dust spreads on a mirror. There are some, whose knowledge is hidden like–an embryo within a womb. See, the knowledge of some people is evident in nine months, and some people might take nine lives for their knowledge to become evident. The lyricist is saying that when dirt settles over a mirror, first we rub it, then we throw water on it, then we polish it. This can take 10 minutes, 20 minutes, or even half an hour. The time it takes to clean the mirror depends on the type of mirror. The third thing, which is most beautiful is that if there is ash on a piece of burning coal, then we cannot touch it. Then, how do we clean it? Only, one breath is needed to clean it. We can blow once and the ash will be cleared, the coal will become free of ash, and the flame will become brighter. The Gita is a unique book. What can I say? I have been giving discourses on the Gita since so long, but it still seems that the meaning of the Gita is not fully clear to me. It is a fathomless ocean.

So, then some people need only a breath of air, and some people may need nine months also, and some people might take nine lives also. Otherwise, keep sitting here. Some people are unfortunate. Those people who do not come to the discourse have been told by some people that they should not go to listen to the discourse. They are unfortunate people, it is their misfortune, what else can I say? Understand one thing very well. All the relations in this world are selfish ones. Only your relation with God is without any selfish motives. Only your relation with God is true. He does not want anything from you. What can be said about human beings, here the sages and saints are also not without selfishness-

Sur nar muni sabki yeh niti, swarth laage kare sab priti
Maat kahe mero poot sapoot, bahini kahe mero sundar bhaiya
Pita kahe mero he kuldipak lok mein maan adhik badaiya.
Patni kahe mero pran pati, jinke jaake main lehun balaiya.
Kahe kavi sun shah akbar jag ki gaanth safed rupaiya.

(Everyone here is the same, everyone loves due to some selfishness. The mother says my good son, the sister says my handsome brother. The father says he is the light of my eyes, he will enhance my good name in this world. The wife says this is my husband whom I love. Listen O human being, the biggest thing for everyone in this world is money.)

Everything is governed by selfishness. All the relations are based on selfish motives. Nobody has been able to avoid this selfishness. Then, the human beings are too small to be able to avoid this. Here, only that person will be able to come who wants to attain salvation. One who wants to uplift himself will come here. Otherwise, there is no medicine for that person who can't see beyond himself.

Those people who work keeping the image of God in their mind, if sometimes due to illness are not able to serve God, then a feeling of sorrow arises in their mind that they were not able to serve God. If someone does not have the adequate materials for worship and is not able to worship God, then he also feels sorrowful. What should these people do? Think of God, remember God.

A very beautiful word has been used here. From 'Navdha Bhakti', '**smaran bhakti**' (rememberance devotion) has been taken. You just think of God. If you are lying in the hospital and cannot do anything, just think of God. It does not cost even a single paise. If you cannot do it alone, then do one thing-

"**Sarvatha tadrishi janah.**"

Meaning, join people like you who have faith in God and together remember God. Acharya ji has spoken of four type of company in his books.

"**The best company is of the ever nourishing God Shri Krishna.**"

Only some people are able to get this. Everyone cannot get it. Only very few people are able to get closeness to God. The second type of company that he has spoken of is to keep the company of those people in **whose hearts God has appeared**. Like the Upanishads have told us that though there is fire in every wood, but every wood cannot be used for fuel. Some wood is used to make furniture. Some wood is used to make windows and doors. But in every wood there is the capability of burning. If it is used for fuel then it will light up a fire. "**Similarly every human being has the capability of becoming God.**"

In everyone of those who are sitting here, godliness can manifest itself. In some, it has already manifested itself and in others it is going to manifest itself. It will definitely manifest itself one day, the Upanishads say. "Keep patience." "Keep patience."

What is the third type of company? Tell us O Master. Then, the acharya said – "Keep the company of scriptures." To believe in the scriptures is equal to believing in a saint. The company of scriptures is equal to the company of saints. If you are reading the Upanishads then it is equal to being in the company of saints. If you are reading the Shrimadbhagwat, then you are in the company of Shukdev.

The fourth type of company is described by "**tadrisha janah**" meaning keep the company of a person who has the same amount of devotion as you have. Then, the question comes – how will we benefit from this type of company? See, due to this, if your devotion does not grow, it will not lessen also. Because if two devotees meet, then they will discuss the Lord only, they will not talk about worldly matters.

"**It is in the hands of God to place you in good company, it is in your hands to save yourself from bad company.**"

Good company means, that, which takes you from the wrong path to the right path, which saves you from untruth. Keep the company of one on whose habits and thoughts you have faith. See, nowadays people say, "How do I know what a person is like in truth?" So, do one thing only "**Keep the company of yourself**." If the world talks, let it talk. You don't need the certificate of the world to walk on this path.

"**Don't look at what the world is telling you, think about what God is telling you.**"

See, God means 'your soul'. Whatever your soul says, do that. That is never untrue. If your soul gets peace in doing some work, then definitely do it. If we do something wrong, then we are not able to sleep in the night, we feel restless, we keeping tossing and turning the whole night. When we do some good deed, the mind is peaceful. So, if your soul says that you have done a good deed, then accept what your soul is saying, no matter what the world says.

Because, "**a peaceful mind is the most comfortable pillow.**" So, do such work by which your mind becomes peaceful. The scriptures have said – "Bad company should always be avoided."

"**Jaake sang kubuddhi upaje, parat bhajan mein bhang.**" Meaning, on being in whose company, bad thoughts come into your mind and you move away from the path of devotion, leave such a person immediately, no matter who he may be. Tulsi Baba said to Meera – "**Jake priya na ram vaidehi, tajhi tahi koti vairi**

sam…" Meaning, discard the company of those who do not worship Ram and Sita. So, should we leave our family? See, society will always put obstacles in your path. Your devotion is pure. If your devotion becomes like gold, then you should understand that your family members will oppose you. If the person who is closest to you gets ready to kill you, then understand that your devotion is about to be fulfilled. Now, the time has come to meet God. This incident has happened in the life of Prahlad, it has happened in the life of Vibhishan. When did Vibhishan get Ram, when Ravan who was close to him, kicked him.

"**Tum pitu saras bhale mohi mara ram bhaje hitu nahin tumhara.**" Meaning, Vibhishan said that even though you may kick me, but without going into Ram's shelter, you will not become happy. Now, I am going into Ram's shelter, don't blame me. He could not meet Ram even after seeing Hanuman who was his guru. He met Ram when Ravan kicked him. Prahlad's father came to kill him. Who does not know Meera's history? All these incidents will happen.

Don't keep anyone's company. Keep your own company. Become alone. You become alone.

Jitasano jitshwaso jitsango. Meaning, be alone. Improve yourself, that is enough. If you improve yourself it will also be a very big accomplishment. Don't be disappointed by your efforts. You will definitely get success. Someone will be successful in nine days, someone in nine lives, everyone has their own level. Only do this:

"**Sarvatha sarvbhaven bhajaniyon vrajaadhipa.**" Meaning, the best religion is to worship Shri Krishna with a pure heart. If you are not able to serve God due to illness or poverty, then "**smartvyam, smartvyam**" (Just remember God). Wherever you may be, however you may be, the thought of God should not leave you. Tension, emotions, struggles arise in a human being's mind only when he forgets God. If you keep remembering God always, then no incident will have an influence on your mind.

Yadu Maharaj had asked this question to Dattatreya Maharaj – "How should the mental state of our mind be like?" He said,

"In this sky, the clouds come, lightning strikes, storms come, but does anything happen to the sky?" Yadu Maharaj said, "No, nothing happens to the sky." Then, Dattatreya Maharaj replied, "Son, you become like the sky. Your mental state should be like the sky because the cloud will rain, the lightning will strike, but your mind should remain peaceful. There should be no effect on your mind. Then, the disciple asked, "How will I bring my mind in this state?" He said – "Wherever you are, however you are, don't forget God. **Smartvyam, smartvyam, smartvyam** – never forget him.

Bhaktibhalasha charitanusari dugdhadi chauryen yashobisari
Kumari nandit ghosh naari mam prabhu shri girirajdhari.
Vrijganamvrind sada vihari andomurhangasya tamovihari
Krira rasavaish tamobhisari mam prabhu shri girirajdhari.
Venuswananandit pantgari rasatlal padprachari
Kridanavayasaya kriti daityamaari mam prabhu shri girirajdhari.

See, although we have learned that it is our duty to serve God, but India's sages are not confined to the four walls of the temples. His duty is to come out of the confines of the temple and serve human beings –

"**True religion is that which can be followed.**" Religion is not something that can be defined. Religion is that which saves one from downfall. Religion is that which makes you happy, which makes you enthusiastic, which does not make you worried. The service of the poor, serving the cow, serving the trees, serving the society, this is also religion. Cleaning the temple is not the sole definition of religion. Yes, service can also be of two types – from the physical body and from the spiritual body.

See, yesterday, a question came before me. I became very happy to hear that question. The question was – in Ramayan, there are songs in praise of God (pad) and there are verses (charan). What is the difference between the two?

See, there is a lot of difference between the two. Goswami ji (writer of Ramayan) has used these two forms of poetry after deep thought. "**The songs (pad) are worshipped and the verses (charan) are served.**"

Wherever the word 'pad' has been used, there God has been worshipped. Wherever the word 'charan' has been used, there God has been served. This is the difference between worship and service. "**Worship is with a motive, but service is without any motive.**"

Wherever the word 'pad' has been used, their worship has taken place, for example, the 'kevat' (boatman) episode. The boatman wants that not only him, but his whole family and ancestors should achieve salvation. Behind worship, there is a motive; behind service, there is no motive. The lover is one who acts only to please his lover. If the wife serves her husband, then there is no motive behind that service. She does not have the desire to get anything in return for her service.

Where the word 'pad' has been used, it shows devotion with a motive. So, there is prayer there. God, I am poor and helpless, you are able and strong. I am a sinner, free me from my sins God. Where 'charan' has been used, there is service to God. Meaning, there the human being has prayed. Like Jaidev Maharaj has prayed. See-

"Shrit kamla kuch mandala dhrit kundal ae
Kalit lalit van maal jai-jai dev hare.
Amal kamal dal lochan bhav mochan ae
Tribhuvan bhavan nidhan jai-jai dev hare.

So, Goswamiji has used 'pad' and 'charan' with deep thought.

Nivedanam tu smartvyam sarvatha tadrishairjaneh
Sarveshewarashch sarvatama nijechaatah karishayati.

The Acharya will make it clear in the third verse that if a human being offers everything to God, then what will God do? What will you gain by going into God's shelter? What will we have to do so that our faith in God becomes stronger? If our faith is not becoming stronger, then what is the reason for this?

Come, I will take you into the verses of the Upanishads. In

this, a sage told his disciple that if he wanted to remove the barrier between God and the human soul and reach God, then he needed to –

Vadanti chaitat prapasam nashtam aashtintche daatamvidoti chistah
Tathapi mohyati prayajmanava krit suvismit kritya madantostim

Here, the saint is teaching his disciple, "Son, the world is destructible, it can be destroyed in a minute, it is breakable, but still God's drama is visible in the world in the form of humour in three forms. One, that entices the people who have achieved salvation, one that entices the devotees, one that entices the self. When these three forms are spread in the whole world, then "**Tathapi muhanti tanmayaya**," (Meaning, even big and wise people start considering this world real.) The disciple asked the saint, "Maharaj, tell us some way of rising beyond this magic spell created by God."

See, the spiritual element is not at all difficult. It has been made difficult. It has been said that it is unattainable, immeasurable, incomprehensible, incomparable etc. etc. The wave is the ocean, the ocean is the wave. It is beyond imagination. Then the disciple got scared and asked, "Maharaj, when all this is beyond understanding, then how will I do it? The sage said, "Do as I tell you to." The disciple said, "Maharaj, can I tell you one thing. Don't be angry with me. What you have said is the truth, but it seems to me that the disciple is like a 'fish in water.' Like a fish cannot survive on being removed from water, similarly a disciple cannot survive without devotion. O God, show me some easy path." Then, the sage said, "See, the path that is easy and simple, is a little convoluted." The disciple said, "It does not matter, you tell me. I will do it." Then, the sage said, "Son, '**Suvismitam kritagyam natosmitam**' Meaning, there is only one solution. Bow before him, salute him, worship him, that's all. The human beings cannot be victorious over the worldly desires, so you go into the shelter of the creator of this world. Then, '**Nijechcha**

karishayati,' he will definitely help you, but only when you accept his supremacy.

Sarveshvarashch sarvatama – Meaning, the God who is the lord of everyone, to whom the disciple is praying, when that disciple says, "Maharaj, I am not aware of what is beneficial for me. You are wise, you are able. Should I walk on the path of happiness or the path of renunciation. What is appropriate for me, tell me. Arjun had said-

"Shishyasya te aham shadhimam tvam prapannam."

Meaning, Maharaj, I am your disciple, I am your son. You suggest me a way which is beneficial for me and everyone else. The sage of India does not think only for himself, he asks for everyone–

Shri ji baba ne mahari raksha karo,
tam mastak pe mahare hast dharayo.
Shri ji baba ne swami raksha karo...
Hari bhakti kara sam bhaav dharo,
maharo aasro ek tamari kharo
Mahara shri ji baba ne swami raksha karo...

Sarveshwar sarvatama:

The lord of all human souls, the God of all human souls. See, 'Navratan' has originated from worry. It is said in the second couplet, "Sarveshwar sarvatama," the one who is the lord of everyone. So, when the lord is there, why should the disciple worry? Our lord is fully aware of what is happening in our lives. This means that when he is fully aware of everything, then he wants this event to happen in our life. So, see, never try to give any advice to God because he knows everything. Sometimes, people start saying that very bad times have come, 'kalyug' has come, there is so much sin in this world. When will God take an incarnation? How will everything become alright? Why do you worry? God is omniscient. He knows everything. Why do you worry? It is God's responsibility to look after the world. You don't advice him.

When Lord Ram appeared on this earth, the 'devtaas'

(celestial beings) had prayed to him to come to the earth and help them. God agreed to them. The second time, the 'devtaas' again repeated their mistake. They took Lord Shiva and went to the Kshirsagar (ocean) and said, "God please come and deliver us." God said, "No, this time, I will come when I want to, you go." This earth is the wife of Lord Vishnu, so the husband knows about his wife. So, God heard the prayer of human beings when he took birth on this earth in the form of Krishna, but he acted as he wanted to. Here, acharya ji is using the words 'sarveshwar', 'sarvatama' meaning God knows everything. It is said in the Atharvaveda – "**Hari om hari saakshat, bhagwan shariratma... toyameechyut.**" Meaning, God is imperishable, eternal, all-knowing, he is never separated from his divine powers.

The acharya is saying that when you have surrendered before God, then don't go and tell him that this event is happening in my life, because if it is happening then "**nijechcha karishayati.**" Meaning, it is happening with his will. This does not mean that we should rest on God's powers alone and not do anything ourselves. It does not mean that we should not do business and not do any work. See, God is not saying this. We have to do the karma (action). Karma is the duty of the body. But, we only have to be free from the attachment towards the action. We have to discard the attachment towards the fruit of the action. Do business, but don't think that I will earn money from this business and give happiness to my family. You cannot do this. It is in the hands of God to give happiness or sorrow to your family. Everything happens according to his will.

God is all-knowing, meaning that the positive and adverse circumstances in human life are all given by God. Then, the question arises that what will happen to those people who have not dedicated themselves to God, who have not taken initiation. Does God not do anything for them? To understand this, we will have to show you a passage from the Gita. In the Gita, God said, "Arjun, the human being who is of this type, who indulges in wine and women, who indulges in worldly desires, who is a slave to the senses, he has to wander in birth after birth in the form of dogs and pigs." We have got this human life to do something. Whoever loses this good opportunity, then he will wander birth after birth in the form of those beings who indulge in all worldly desires. Yes, dogs and pigs also indulge in worldly desires. They experience the happiness of eating, sleeping, the happiness of the senses, yes, the animals also get happiness like human beings. Remember, the happiness that the rich man gets on sleeping on a soft mattress, the same happiness a pig gets in sleeping in wet mud. There is no difference in this. So many people come and go away. Only those people make history who achieve something. Everyone does work here, but there way of working is different. You also do devotion, Meera had also done devotion, Surdas had also done devotion, Narsi Mehta had also done devotion. But there ways of doing devotion were different from ours. So, don't give advice to God. Yes, even if you get sorrow, thank God. Say– "God you have not given me food today, it is your will. Due to your blessings, I was able to observe a fast today."

"Koi din mishthan bhojan man bhavta
Koi din aave upvaas, such-dukh to aave sansar maan
Bhavti bhajva bhagwan, such-dukh to..."

'Navrattan' means the nine planets. The first couplet was the Sun. The second couplet was the Moon. The Sun, Moon, and Jupiter are all planets. Today, the talk of difficulties caused by planets has become very prevalent. People search for ways to propitiate the planets. See, the meaning of difficulties caused by the planets is fate. When the planets are troubling you, then do a lot of charity. When misfortune befalls you, when you have to fulfill your heart's desire, then three things are useful – mantras (holy verses), jewels, and medicine. So, when misfortune strikes you, do more charity. Charity is not only of money, charity is of time, of power. Serve with your body, with your time. Remember God. This is also a charity. There are only two solutions for changing your fate – either bear it or do charity. The hand of human beings has been made to give not take. But, today–

"**Sab jaat kujaat bhaye mangta.**" Meaning, everyone has become a beggar. Some are begging on the streets and some are wearing ties and suits and begging.

Today, in the second couplet, we are able to see the Moon. This couplet is a pearl. The jewel of the Moon is the pearl. Here, 'smaran bhakti' (devotion through rememberance) is the pearl. With this pearl, the pain caused by the planets will lessen. Secondly, you will not go through emotional upheavals. Thirdly, in the form of mantras, you will remember God. Whoever is your God, you will remember him. See, there is nothing which is needed to do 'smaran bhakti.' For 'yagnas' (worship ritual) and charity, you need money. For remembering God, you only need your mind. Like Prahlad had done. He said to his father – What is in you, is in me. What is in me, is in you. What is below is up. What is up is below. What is left is right. What is right is left. So, God is present equally everywhere. We should not forget his powers. Don't forget the nature of God, his form. What is the form of God like?

"**Komal chit ati deen dayala, karan binu raghunath kripala**
Geedh adham khag aamish bhogi, gati dinhi jo jachat yogi."

Meaning, O Brother, see the nature of God. He is so kind that he confers spiritual bliss, even to those who eat meat, such as, 'Jataayu', who is a carnivorous bird. (Ramcharitmanas) The yogis also yearn for this kind of a spiritual–achievement. The only condition is that one should dedicate oneself to God. One should have the feeling, that what is God's will be done. As God sees fit, I don't have any desire. I don't have any want. Your will is my will –

"**We are agreeable to that which is your will.**"

Prahlad and Gajendra have done ('Smaranam Bhakti') remembrance devotion. At his last moment, Gajendra remembered God by offering a lotus which was symbolic of his heart. God has said, "Arjun, at the last moment of his life, if the human soul does not remember me due to cough, fever, or ill-health, then I will remember him."

"Ajamil ko ant samay mein tera naam jab yaad aaya
Shri radhe govinda gopala tera pyaara naam hai..."

In the fourth verse, Vallabhacharya has said clearly "**Nijechchaat karishayati**," he will do according to his will. But, human beings today do not have patience. Some people pray using the beads of the rosary, but if their desires are not fulfilled, they throw away the rosary. Keep faith, keep patience. In both Chagan and Magan a desire to renounce the world arose. They started meditating beneath the 'peepal' (the holy fig tree) tree. Narad ji came and asked them what they were doing. Both of them said that they were meditating. We want to see God. Narad ji said that it was not so easy to see God. It would take them as many lives as there were leaves on the fig tree. Go home, enjoy yourself, you will get nothing by renunciation. Chagan heard this and went away. Narad asked Magan, "Why are you still sitting?" He said, "After as many lives as there are leaves on this tree, I will get God, isn't it? So, I will keep meditating till I get God." So, you should have this kind of patience. How he will give, when he will give, this only God knows. When sorrow comes into your life, you should think that the sins of the past lives have lessened. And when happiness comes into your life, then you should think that the good deeds of the previous lives are being lessened. So, don't get disheartened by sorrow. There is only way to escape sorrow....

Shriman narayan, narayan, narayan
aadi narayan narayan narayan
Dwarkadheesh ki jai, sadguru devki jai,
om namo parvati pataye
Har har mahadev hare,
jai-jai shri radhe –3
Shrivrindavan bihari lal ki jai.

Meaning, say Shriman narayan, narayan, narayan aadi narayan narayan narayan, Glory be to Dwarkadhessh, glory be to the noble guru, glory to be Shiva and Parvati, Glory be to Mahadev, glory be to Shri Radhe, Glory be to the one who lives in Vrindavan.

✻ CHAPTER 3 ✻

Shri Vallabhacharya says-

"**Sarvesham prabhu sambandho na pratyekmiti stithiah**
Atontaya viniyogeapi chinta ka swasaya sopi chet."

–Third couplet

The Lord Shri Krishna is a person who belongs to the human beings. He is a well-wisher of the human beings. The nature of God is merciful, benevolent, one who loves equally all living things. When the devotee is standing in front of God, then God does not ask how educated you are, how much wealth do you have? What is your caste? Which nation do you belong to? There is only one relation with God and that is of love. God does not form any other relation except that of love. Human beings have formed relations with the world. The world is incomplete, its broken, its destructible, so the relation with it is also broken, its destructible.

The meaning of love is 'surrender'. There are no calculations in love. That works in business only. Here there is surrender, there is faith, there is humility, there is emotion. For making deals and for doing business, ability is needed. For love, emotion is needed, madness is needed. God does not look at caste, creed, family, wealth, or cleverness. God looks at the heart only. The scriptures say that whenever a being formed a relation with the world, he had to cry. With that eternal, indestructible, and limitless one love is permanent and mutual. God has said – **'Yeh yathaamam prapadyante taansthtaiva bhajaamyaham.'** Meaning, with the emotion that a being forms a relation with me,

I also form a relation with him with that emotion. Even though the behaviour of God may be difficult to understand, but he loves everyone equally–

Jaati-paati kul dharm badai dhan, bal, parijan, gun, chaturai.
Kah raghupati sunu yamini bata manhun ek bhagti kar naata.

Meaning, no matter how a being may be, if he comes in front of me, then I will make him gold. Not only this, I will make him like myself. Nabhaji has said in 'Bhaktmal'-

Bhakti bhakt bhagwat....chaturnam vapu ek

Meaning, God and devotee are playing the same roles. There is no difference between Krishna and gopi. Krishna is gopi, and the gopi is Krishna. The one who is God is the devotee and the God. There is no difference between the two.

Bhakt bhagwan mein yadi antar hua to prem nahi
Preet jahan pardo nahin par do vahan nahin preet
Preeti kare pardo rakhe ye to dushman ki reet.

Meaning, where there is difference between the devotee and God, that is not love. Where there is love, there is no barrier. If there is a barrier, that is not love. To love and still keep a barrier, that is the sign of an enemy.

The king of the whole world, the one who loves his devotees, when that God showers his blessings on the beings, he does it equally. Now, the couplet which we are going to describe, there the equality of all living things in God's eyes is clearly evident. God is the father of the world. The water-dwelling beings, the land-dwelling beings, the sky-dwelling beings are all his children. No one is insignificant or special for him.

"Inequality is the reason for all sin."

In the method of yoga, it is said that till we exist, ego cannot be discarded. Even when there is knowledge, ego will be there. If ego is not there, you are also not there. Bhagwati Shruti says '**pragyanam vaham.**' Meaning, the melting away of ego is meditation. If some feeling of ego and myself still remains, then the meditation will not be complete. There are different types of meditation. In front of God, the gopis said – O Krishna! We have not only discarded our sons, husbands, wealth, and family, we have discarded all worldly desires and come to you. God, are we not fit for you. God, why don't you appear now? God is merciful and benevolent. Everyone is equal in his eyes.

Who can remove the worry of the devotees except a true guru. The Vedas have said that the time of a good guru must be spent in the devotees "**samyak bhranti bhanjanam** to remove the doubts of devotees**.**" Dave ji is sitting at the feet of the guru. He is worried, there are emotional upheavals in his mind, he is hesitating, he is not able to speak. So, the guru asked – Speak, what is your worry? He said, "O Master! Who am I? I don't even know this, then how will I know how is the one whom I am going to serve. **Koham? Kenaham? Kasyaham?** Meaning, Who am I? Whom do I belong to? Then, what is the relation between Him and me? Tell me this also. Maharaj, I am worried every second. I spend my whole day in carrying out my worldly duties. Will my whole life be spent in this? If my whole life is spent in this, then how will I go back to God's house with my empty hands? To look after and feed my family, to fulfill the obligations of the society, and if I get some free time, to spend it in discussing unimportant things, is this how my life will be spent? Now, what should I do? I don't even know this. God, when I have come into your shelter, then I know I should not worry about food. But, God we worldly people, no matter how hard we try, we can't stop worrying. Due to this worry, we are not able to concentrate fully in serving you. While serving God, tears don't come into our eyes. God, when there is no enjoyment in a task, then why should I do that task? Guru ji, you are able, tell me why this is happening with me. A good guru is kind, is merciful, there is only one thing in his mind that my disciple should benefit in whatever way possible. Recently, when I was abroad, someone asked me, "Why do you accept such a person as your disciple whose eating habits are not appropriate, whose habits are not correct? See, brother, one whose eating habits and lifestyle are appropriate, he is already a devotee of God, he does not need a guru as much as a person who is wandering here and there, who is fallen. I know that 500 years before our great guru had forbidden us to accept such people as disciples. But, O guruji, where will such a fallen person go. He cannot do his own welfare, then even if I don't help him, then what will happen to him?

Heri mane prabhu kirtan ka rang hajo,
ang ang bhakti no sang rahjo
Mane vaishnav to satsang hajo
mahara shri ji ne swami raksha karo
Mam mastak par tam hast dharyo.

Once, in a discourse in Uttar Pradesh, five-six such people came to join as my disciples who were evil and bad-charactered. They were not respected in the society. When I accepted them as my disciples, then the people said something. But when I accepted them as my disciples, I said to them that I would take 'dakshina' (gift given by a disciple to his guru) from them, and I would take that from them in a lonely place. Then the people thought that when alone, maybe he would take an envelope containing cash from them. But, when they came to see me alone, they took out their revolvers and put them in front of me. This was my 'dakshina,' then why should I not accept them as my disciples. Otherwise, the devotees can serve the Lord themselves, in their own way. God, himself says that "**jaati-paati kul dharm badai**" (caste, creed, family lineage, religion, and status) I don't look at all these because however a being may be, he is my son. Like worldly parents also wait in the hope that one day my wayward son will come back to me, similarly, God is also standing in wait for you.

Mamaivasho jeev lok jeevbhoot sanatanah

Meaning, however fallen a person may be, on coming into God's shelter, he becomes pure. A person is spoiled by the company he keeps. A person's nature is formed by the company he keeps. As the company is, so are the qualities, as are the qualities, so is the nature. If you don't get good company, then don't keep any company. Be alone. '**Dusang sarvatha tyajaya.**'

Meaning, bad company should always be discarded. It can corrupt you in a moment, like it did to Ajamil. Otherwise what has been spoilt today, can be improved also tomorrow. If someone has done a bad deed once, he does not become a sinner forever. Everyone can improve. That is why God had freed Ahilya from her sins. All this is a reassurance for us. That is why God delivered Valmiki from his sins, he delivered Sugreev. If God had closed the doors for them, then what would have been the use of this life for them? God says that however a being may be, he is mine.

So, the sadguru looked at Dave ji and said – Dave ji, why do you worry? God loves everyone equally, and he looks at everyone equally. Does God love Arjun and not Duryodhan? If this is so, then we don't want such a God. God loves both of them. But, he has to behave differently with both of them. Like you love your wife, son, mother equally, but behave differently towards all of them. If a sick person goes to a doctor, the doctor will treat him, so that the disease does not spread further. The doctor does not have any enemity with the sick person. His only concern is to cure his patients' disease. This does not mean that he does not love them. See, although this has not been shown clearly in the Ramayan, but those who have read it know that when God lifted his bow to kill the demons, he had tears in his eyes. These tears were because he had to kill a living being. If God strikes you, he saves you also. At the tip of the arrow, he had kept the fruit of salvation, and who is fortunate enough to get a death as that of Ravan. What was Ravan's condition at the time of death? In his eyes was Lord Shiva, on his lips was Lord Ram's name, and in his heart was Sita ji. Who gets a death like this? When God drew up the arrow, there were tears in his eyes. He had no enmity with Ravan, he was against the ideology of Ravan.

Dave ji, why do you think that you have to worry? "**Nij ichcha deen dayala**" Meaning, God says that everything is happening as per my wish. Come, I will remove your worry –

Sarvesham prabhu sambandho...

Meaning, God has an equal relationship with everybody.

'Navrattan' was begun with the word 'worry'. Again and again, God reminds you that the person who has dedicated himself to God, should not worry. Remember, when you form a relation with God, you don't surrender only yourself before God, you surrender both the soul and the body. Soul means the ego and body means the physical body. Me, my wife, son-daughter and my house, property, wealth all belong to God now. God exists not only in the physical form, but also in the soul. Only tying a thread in your neck is not forming a relation with God. Dedication to God means that everything is being surrendered. There are no options that I will give this and I will not give this. When God recited the 'Chatushlokibhagwat', which had four couplets to Brahmdev, he said in the second couplet –

"**Brahmdev I am everywhere, I am forever, I am equal for everyone**." Whatever you can see in this world is nothing else but God.

"**Ishawasasya idam sarvam yat kinchit jagatyam jagat.**"

Meaning, when there is nothing else but God, then I am also God. "**Krishnoaham**," I am Krishna. The acharya is telling here that a relation with God is forever and equal. There is no smallness or bigness in it. So, if God has an equal relation with everyone, then this devotee who is dedicating himself to God, what will he get? See, human being is such a being who either acts due to some selfish motive or acts due to fear. So, he asks what is the benefit of surrendering everything to God? The guru said, "By surrendering everything, you will be saved from two things. One is the feeling of I, myself, and the other is the feeling of pride in yourself. When there is no mine, then there is no yours. When mine and yours is removed, only ours is left. Till the feeling of I, myself is there, desire will also be there. Remember, that in this couplet, you have to guard yourself against escapism. Where there is hope, disappointement will also be there. Till now we have only learnt that what God is doing, he is doing right. He is making me do things. I have offered myself and mine all to him. Now, I don't have anything–

This body is not mine, it is given by someone else
The one who has given it has given it with such grandeur
The one who has taken it says with pride that it is mine
This body...
Live life thinking this to be the secret of life
On the path of meditation, this is a means of
devotion given by someone
This body...

Krishna tavaasmi, Krishna tavaasmi, Krishna tavaasmi. Meaning, God, I am yours. Everything that belongs to me is yours. First is equality; then is I, myself. The pride in your power, your house - discard all these feelings. It is the habit of human beings to write their names everywhere. Wherever he gives a little bit of charity, he gets his name written there. This demonstration is nothing else but pride. See, don't demonstrate your devotion also. Pray to God also alone. If you worship in the open then pride can come into you, then your devotion may decrease. Do your prayers in front of God. He is the only one who needs to see it. What will you do with a certificate by the society? If it gives a certificate now, it may take it away later.

"**There are only two obstacles in the path of salvation, ego and attachment.**"

"This is mine"–this is attachment. "I have done this"–this is ego. This feeling of ownership is ego. '**Na mam**,' '**na mam**' (nothing is mine) when you will say this, then only will ego and attachment go away. If you want to conquer the feeling of mine, then spread this feeling more – everything is mine or nothing is mine. So, the acharya is saying that when nothing belongs to you, everything belongs to God, then God will worry himself. Why do you worry? When you have discarded the feeling of ownership, then ego is finished. I have got this hospital constructed, I have got this school constructed – this is ego. When God has mercy on his subjects, he takes away money, wisdom, position, and prestige from them. Vritasur explained this to Indra in the Shrimadbhagwat. **When 'I' will die, then only God will become**

visible. 'Mine' exists till you have something. When you don't have something, then the feeling of 'mine' will also die. See, the devotees don't have anything, that is why they don't worry. There is a saying, "Prevention is better than cure." So, if God has mercy on you, he will not give you the disease of worldly possessions. He will give birth to you at a poor man's house, like Narsi Mehta.

To mahara gopi chandan tulsi hai jo haar
Sancho naam mahara sanwaro re...
Mahari daulat ya jhanjaro pakhaj re shyamada girdhari
Ae maharo ek tamaro adhaar re shyamada girdhari
Mahari hundi sweekaro maharaj re shyamada girdhari
Rahwa na thi jhupidi aur jimwa na thi jwar
Log kare de khekadi na thi shyamal sa seth hun naam re
Shyamada girdhari...

God said to Indra that the person on whom he has mercy, he takes away money, prestige, position, wisdom everything from him. Only then his pride is removed.

Till there is ego and the feeling of 'mine,' till then the person cannot even serve God. Today, I have to start serving. You must all have served God. There are some things about serving God, which everyone does not know. Yes, some people might know. Today's new generation does not have the knowledge of why they should serve God and how they should serve God.

It is happening due to our traditions, so we also do it. But, today's young generation does not accept anything merely because it is tradition. Today, in this age of e-mail, there is not that much faith in the children. Without understanding themselves, they are not going to do it only due to faith. Today, is not the age of 500 years before, the age of our great acharya.

Here, in the third and fourth verse of the third couplet, '**archanam bhakti**' is being stated. Who can serve God? Where there is no selfishness, only those can serve God. Where there is selfishness, worship will be there. There is difference between serving God and worshipping him. The word 'worship' that has come in the Vedas, that word 'worship' may seem to be synonymous with service, but among the devotees, there is a difference between service and worship. In the '**pushti**' community, service has a separate meaning. Here, we have to reach till the role of the acharya. For serving God, it is necessary to be free from ego and attachment. I don't have anything, everything belongs to God. Only by discarding this feeling of attachment, one can serve God. I am just an accountant. I am just a trustee of God's property. You should have this feeling. Then, the question arises that when everything belongs to God, then how can I use it. And when the body is there, needs will also be there. So, the acharya has assured us-

"Sarvesham prabhu sambandho na pratyekamiti stithiah
Atoanyaviniyogeapi chinta ka swaroop soapi chet (3)"

Meaning, that what you have offered God, that has now become sacred. You can use it now. It is a sacred thing now. If you use it without selfish motives, then there is no worry, there is no obstacle to that. But, if you use it thinking that it should benefit me only, I don't care what happens to the others, then it becomes a crime.

What is the feeling of dedication in a human soul like? Say, "**Krishna tavaasmi**" "**Krishna dasoaham.**" (I belong to Krishna, I am Krishna's servant). The complete renunciation of ego and attachment is possible only by this feeling. And without discarding ego and attachment, service is not possible.

Come, I will show you that a person who may not have served God like us, but who has served the society unselfishly, he also becomes free from ego and attachment. He becomes a yogi without any attachment or selfishness. When Bhishma was lying on a bed of arrows, at the time of his death, he said to God and the Pandavas – I have been able to save myself from ego and attachment, the reason for this is:

"Iti mati rup kalpita vitrishna bhagwati saatwat pungawe vibhumni swa sukhbhupgate kwachit vihaartum..."

So, when you have dedicated yourself, then what happens. "**Chinta ka swastha soapi chet.**" This was spoken by God.

When Arjun said to Krishna that these are my uncles, brothers, and gurus, how can I lift my bow on them, how can I be happy after killing them, God said –

**"Jatasya hi dhruvo mrityu janam dhruvo mritasaya ch
Tasmatapariharaye arthe nanu shochanti pathita."**

(Bhagwad Gita)

So, "**Ka paridevna**" tell me Arjun. Meaning, "What is the worry, tell me Arjun." Here, everyone has to go. You are just a means of getting things done. This is what the acharya is saying "**Chinta ka swasth soapi chet.**" So, "**Ka paridevna**," Arjun, what is the worry? Dave ji, from here '**archanam bhakti**' (reverent worship) starts. What is the meaning of serving God –

**"Sushshen chadev yen sevasaya sukham
bhavati paritushyati ch"**

Meaning, the God whom you are serving, the action with which you get happiness and satisfaction, that is service. Service is successful because it is done with an unselfish attitude. In worship, there is expectation. So, God does not accept your worship, and service is selfless. So, God accepts it. This has happened in the lives of many devotees. God himself is free from all illness. Worship is done of all Gods and Goddesses. The Vedas tell us that there is a seed mantra for each God and Goddess, which if you recite for a specified number of times, then that God or Goddess will have to appear in front of you and will have to fulfil your wish. In service, whatever action we do, it is not done for one's own self. If the one you are serving becomes happy, then the service was successful, and the worship was successful.

**"In worship, there is an order;
in service, there is a request."**

Before entering into service, it is necessary to know that only doing 'aarti' and offering a meal (bhog lagana) to God is not service. With worship, you bring a God or Goddess under your control; whereas by service, you give bliss to God. Service is of two types. One is service by resources and the other is service by self. God has said that the two types of service are - one is that you discard the pride of action or you discard the desire for a fruit. Here, service is of two types – one is by body and one is by wealth. In the second type, people get service done by giving money, for example, getting a hospital constructed somewhere. Some rich people keep a 'pandit' for the service of God. It is alright. There is no restriction on keeping a 'pandit' to serve God, but if service is done ourselves, then it is the best service. Even if you do it for 10 minutes, but do it yourself. Sit before God yourself and talk to him. Tell God that I am busier today; I was not able to sit with you. God, do one thing, when I go to work, you also come with me. Come and sit in my heart. Sit in my hands –

"**Bar bar raghuvir sambhari tarakeyu pavan tanay balbhari,**
Jehi giri charan deyi hanumata tehi jo ga paatal turanata."

Meaning, when I do an action, you look after me. When some people go outside, they take God's idol with them. It is a good thing. But, instead of taking the idol with you, take God in your heart. Could Hanuman who was able to lift up the mountain, not take a idol of God with him? But, no, he took God in his heart. These gopis also while doing their household duties keep God in their mind.

Shukdev ji has said –

"**Vaam baahu krit vaam kapolo valgitbhrudharirpit venu**
Komalagulibhirashrit margah gopyaishyati yatra mukund."

Mother Yashoda at the time of doing her household duties would remember God and sing devotional songs. Where you cannot use wealth to serve God or serve Him yourself, then serve by your mind. When your body doesn't work, do this. Once, a mother asked me, "Son, I am not able to sit even in '**sukhasan** (yogic posture),' then how can I serve God?" So, I said, "Sit on a stool or a chair." The mother said, "Son, then God will be seated below me. This will be inappropriate." I said, "Mother, when there is love, then this does not matter." Understand one thing. Keep your behaviour with your neighbour cordial, otherwise he will not forgive you. My lord forgives you also and forgets everything also. But, you serve with your mind, if you cannot do it with your body. But, remember in mental service, worldly feelings should not come in, otherwise, the service will be spoilt. The meaning of mental service is not that you have recited the name of God 108 times, and mentally offered sweets to him. The meaning of mental service is

"Chetas tat pranmam seva."

Meaning, our mind should be immersed in God. Yes, this was the problem of Arjun also that his mind was very fickle. How could this problem be solved – "**Chanchal hi man Krishna...**" (Meaning, Krishna, my mind is fickle.) This problem is very difficult to solve. Krishna said –

"Abhyasen tu kaunteya."

Meaning, Arjun, everything is possible by practice. Practice continuously. You will certainly be successful. God has given two solutions to achieve concentration – '**Swadhyaya aur kirtan**,' meaning study and recitation. In student life, to remember something, first we read it, that is '**swadhyaya**' and then we write it so that our memory becomes permanent. Here also, first is '**swadhyaya**' (reading) and then '**kirtan**' (recitation).

"Swadhyaya is reading and kirtan is writing." So, to write God's name on your heart, recite his name again and again.

Mero radharaman girdhari girdhari shyam banwari-3

Focussing your attention on God is mental service. The definition of service is – "**Maam agya.**" (Meaning, order me God.) Two things are included under service to God. How will my Lord get happiness, how will my Lord get bliss? The definition of happiness is also different. This only the person knows what will make him happy. So, the human being says that God you order me, what can I do for you. Remember, when you install an idol, then godliness comes itself. Whether it is an idol given by the guru, or even if it is not given by an able guru, even then God's idol should be installed. Whether the idol is of mud, brass, wood, gold, or silver, everything is acceptable. The idol of God should be installed and served. "An idol is the incarnation of God himself." It is the order of the guru –

"**Paricharyam sadakuryat**" because "**Dhruv tatv yastidam.**" Meaning, the moment an idol is installed, God enters into that idol. It is an incarnation of God himself and Bhagwati Shruti says – "**Yatha dehe tatha deve**" (where there is an idol, God himself is there). As a human soul looks after his body, similarly God should be worshipped. As you feel warm, God must also feel warm. If you feel cold, then God must also feel cold. An idol is an incarnation of God himself. Don't think it to be an idol of stone. Like we feel hungry and thirsty, similarly God also feels hungry and thirsty. As your child does not sleep without hearing the lullaby, similarly God will also not be able to sleep without hearing the lullaby. So, sing–

Gopal maharo palan mein jhule re, nandlal maharo...

Previously, mothers used to make their children sleep in cradles and used to carry on their household tasks. As a mother runs after the child with a cup of milk and the child pretends that he does not want to drink the milk, similarly, you have to cajole God to take the meal offered to him. Offering a meal to God is not a mere formality. If you take 20-25 minutes to eat your food, then how will God eat his food in five minutes? Serve the idol with emotion. This is a manifestation of God. Ask God everyday –

Maam agya path – Meaning, God order me, how should I serve you. How should I give happiness to you?

By worship, you are able to control God. By service, you have to make God happy. In worship, there is deal making. In service, there is no deal making. So, in worship, God does not appear and accept your worship. But, in service, God himself appears and accepts your service. It is said in the scriptures –

Hariom yasmat stitho yatmapi kathmapi
Karvaapi bahatmuchyate gopikesh
kamalhaste charu hasam karoti.

Meaning, who accepts the sweets offered by the gopis with his own hands? The question must have arisen in your mind that we also serve God, but God never accepts anything from us. He accepts. You have not understood. See, you pluck a flower and then weigh it. Then smell it. Then after smelling, you weigh it. There will be no difference in its weight. But, haven't you smelled the flower. You have, but the weight of the flower has not decreased. God also takes like this, but he does not lessen. Instead, he increases with his benevolent sight. God is kind. He knows that if something belonging to this human being lessens, he might feel deprived. Otherwise, tomorrow you will stop offering anything to God. So, he does not let the offering lessen. Otherwise, he does not even eat.

Na punyam na papam na saukhyam
Na mantron na tirtham na veda na yagya
Aham bhojanam naiv bhojyam na bhokta
Chidanand rup shivoaham shivoaham...

Krishna himself says – "**Naham bhakshitanvamb sarvemithyamishansinan,**" meaning, Mother, I don't eat.

Now, the question comes that we have sacrificed ego and attachment, and we have understood the definition of service and worship. Now, before we can enter into service, obstacles come in our path. Now, we have realised what service is. What should the emotion behind service be? What is the fruit of service? Now, how should we conquer the obstacles that come in the path of service? For this, we will delve into the Upanishads –

Nidraya lok vaartaya shabdade atamvismrite
Shachonavsaram datva chintyaatmankatmani.

The guru has accepted all the things written in the Vedas. He has written discourses on the Upanishads. He has studied the six scriptures. Two things put an obstacle in the service. One is sleep and the other is criticism. The meaning of sleep is laziness. The enemy of human beings is laziness. It does not let us move forward. The second is criticism, meaning, speaking ill or well about someone in his or her absence. Sometimes, the proof of the eyes is also wrong.

See, in Mahabharat, Duryodhan was not able to see even after having eyes. He mistook the land for water and water for land. Only Duryodhan made this mistake because he was without wisdom. Nobody else made this mistake.

The second obstacle is – idle talk. Usually, people indulge in useless talk. This happened to this person, and this person is doing this. The government of Delhi is going to fall. What do you have to do with these discussions? See, in Ramayan, Manthara said – "**Kou hohu nrip hame ka hani, cheri chandi na hui hai rani,**" meaning, how will it matter to me who sits on the throne, I will remain a servant only whoever sits on the throne. So, the Vedas say – "**Vyarth charcha, vyarth chintan, vyarth cheshta** (useless talk, useless thoughts, useless efforts)." You should guard against all three of these. These three put obstacles in the service. Where do you have the free time? If you get busy in talking about the world, then how will you be able to give happiness to God?

Shabdadeh, the meaning of this is one who is ruled by the senses. The person who gives more happiness to his body, how will he give happiness to God? "**The person whose food is tasty, he cannot do devotion.**" This does not mean that you do not provide comforts to yourself. I have forbidden extreme happiness because those who worship the body cannot worship God. To fulfill the senses is equal to becoming a slave of the senses. Till you keep satisfying your senses, the desires will remain awakened and your mind will remain concentrated on indulgence. So, the sages have forbidden this in the Upanishads.

The fourth thing is – to forget oneself. Why has God given this human body to me? What is God's goal behind this? This body has been given because there is intelligence in this body. The faculty of logic is in this body. If God comes in front of us, then we will be able to recognise him. But, if God comes in front of a dog, he will not be able to recognise him. If you are not in your senses, you may commit a crime. God has given you the Vedas, the Bhagwat, but you have not read them. What answer will you give when you go in front of God? The donkey does not have enough intelligence, so he is not reading the Bhagwat, so he is not committing any crime. You have been given the human body, intelligence. If you still do not do it, you will commit a crime.

Apradh paramparavritam na hi mata samupekshate sutam,
Matsamah paatki nasti papaghni twatasma na hi,
Avum gyatva mahadevi yatha yogyam tatha kuru.

Meaning, you cannot even make the excuse that you were not able to understand it. God will ask then why didn't you seek the feet of the great men from where you could get knowledge? This is a crime. So, the sages say – "**Atamvismritey**," meaning, you have forgotten your true self.

It is your duty to make God happy. It is the duty of the son to make the father happy with his character. Gopis do this. There is only one thing in their minds that God should become happy with me. They prepare curd for God only. They serve the cows for God only. They eat food for Krishna only. Krishna is in their heart, in their eyes. This does not mean that you should not live in the society. You have to achieve God while remaining in your human form. You have got the human body for this. You can satisy God by this only and make him happy.

Aaj kari le kamani hari naam ne re
Ae ji aavo avsar tame naahi man manvi re
Kari le...
Bhav bhavni bhakhat bhamashe re,
Are aashe taru kalyan halya marvire. Kari le...
Maya na khel jhuta jan ri re
Sanchu hari naam halya manvi re, kari le...
Deh ki jeev jaave jhuth shere kari le...

Sometimes when a person falls sick, he remembers God. O Lord of the gopis! O King of Dwarka! O Kanha! Mother Kunti said to God –

Vipadah santu nah shashavtatra tatra jagadguro
Bhavto darshanam yatsyad punarbhav darshanam.

Meaning, Mother Kunti said that many great misfortunes came into my life, due to which I had the opportunity to see you many times.

The knowledge of sorrow is called wisdom. The bookish knowledge is not useful at the time of death. Only wisdom is useful. It is written in the Vishnu Puran-

"Sa vidya ya vimuktaye."

Meaning, knowledge leads to liberation. Who worships God? One, those who are sad and the other who are curious. What is this God? How is he? Where does he stay? The curious people want to find an answer to these. Those people who want something also worship God. Those people who want wealth, worship God. But, if they get wealth, they are caught in the desire for more wealth. Those who are knowledgable also worship God. These 'gopis' are knowledgeable, although Raskhan may call them the daughters of cowherds. They are not illiterate. They are extremely knowledgeable. They have gained knowledge. Remember – **To obtain God, you don't need knowledge, but emotion. You don't need brains, but purity. To reach God, you don't need bookish knowledge, but madness.**

Narad ji said in the Bhakti Sutra – **When the greatness of God is realised, then love for God becomes stronger**. When the knowledge about the greatness of a person, thing, or subject is realised, then respect and love for it increases. And when the knowledge of greatness of a person is not realised, then there is no love there. God is kind, merciful. The gopis know this. So, we have realised God's greatness. How do we have to serve him? To know this, listen –

When you wake up in the morning, and when you go to sleep at night, say this only "**Naath tavaasmi, naath dasoaham.**" Meaning, God, I am yours; God, I am your servant. Go to sleep keeping this thought in mind, and when you wake up, say this first of all –

**"Krishna tavaasmi! Krishna dasoaham!
Krishna dasoaham!"**

Meaning, I belong to Krishna. I am Krishna's servant.

If you keep reminding him about this again and again, he will not leave you. Because if he is your God and if you leave him, then this will not cause any ill-fame to God. But, if he is your God, and if he leaves you, then this will cause God ill-fame. So, "Naath tavaasmi, naath tavaasmi, Krishna dasoaham." Belong to

God, and God will look after you himself. Start this chant as soon as morning begins. As soon as you open your eyes, keep God's image in front of your eyes. Or otherwise, remember that form of God whom you are serving. When you start with "Krishna tavaasmi" then you should have faith both in God's name and form. Till you don't have faith in the name of God, till then you will not be able to do devotion. Remember –

"The desire to enjoy the world is a cause of bondage, the desire to worship God is devotion."

"Sa param prem rupa." In the 'Narad Bhakti Sutra', Narad ji says that attraction towards God is like supreme love. So, the image of God should come in your eyes, and "naath tavaasmi" should be on your lips. As soon as you keep your right toe on the ground, then at the time of touching the earth, recite this mantra –

"Uddhritasi varahen krishnen shat bahuna
Dhara devi namastubhyam padsparsh kshamasvame."

Meaning, God has taken the earth out of the 'Varah avtaar', so the earth is the wife of Vishnu. This is mentioned in the third paragraph of the 'Bhagwati Shruti' in Vrat Lila. So, this earth is the wife of Vishnu. I am keeping my impure feet on this earth. So, mother earth, forgive me. See, otherwise, the human body has been considered to be very pure amongst all the species, because only in this body there is the capability to think. It is not there in any other species. If we see it from the physical point of view, then no part of the human body is of any use after death, that is why it is sacrificed to the fire as it is. Whereas the bodies of other species are of multiple uses after death. With the tears of the cow, a medicine is made. In the saliva of the cow, there is the power to fight germs. In the dung and urine of the cow also there are medicinal values. The skin of the animals is also used. Their bones are used. No part of a human being's body is of any use, so it is burnt. So, when we keep our feet on mother earth, we ask for forgiveness. Forgive me mother. So, you should not urinate or defecate wherever you wish, on mother earth. When we call the earth our mother, then we should respect her in the same way.

Then, sit at one place with a peaceful mind and remember Vallabhacharya–

Vande shri Vallabhacharya charananabazam yugalam ch
Yeh to vindye vrijadhish padambujam madhyavaham.

Meaning, remember Vallabhacharya Maharaj. If he was not there, then who would have taken a stupid person like us to God. Our repeated salutes in the feet of such an acharya. After this, remember your guru, whoever he may be.

Trahi shambho jagannath yosansar bahimana
Dagdaham mamta dhrishtam ch yadiyansh gantargatam.

In Sanskrit, the one who does good is called Shankar. Here, we are the ones who burn with the three kinds of fire, and we are remembering our guru. Your service has begun, now remember the Lord of the Gopis –

"**Vaame kare bhudminindram ch sadhvasam giristrum**
Dharyantam mahamvande jitam gopishu gopiyam."

Meaning, O, cowherd who takes the cows out for grazing, the one who helped the gopis, O God!, we salute you again and again.

We remembered the acharya, we remembered our good guru, then we remembered God; now, we have to go and serve him. Before this we should become pure. We have said the mantra for performing our ablutions, now we have to brush our teeth. The teeth were brushed with vegetables before. So, salute the vegetables –

Vanaspataye namasyam vaddhrite swasya shuddhe
Krishna sevarth karyeshu mukham mein vinlipabhuah.

Meaning, O vegetables, before I go to serve Lord Krishna, you purify my mouth. After this, you have to go to the bathroom. So, you should take the pledge that you will recite the mantra for whichever day it is –

Adyapi somvasare mam paap dukhshay
Shri Krishna preetyartham sakal karmadikaraat seva
Siddhyateeshch pratsnanam aham karishaye.

Meaning, why am I going to have a bath. I have purified my mind by thinking of my guru and God. Now, I am going to purify my body. So, at the time of filling water in the bucket, remember the pure rivers, the seven oceans and recite the mantra –

Pushkaradyani tirthani gangadyam saristatha
Agachantu pavitrani samkale sadamam
Shri Krishna Vallabh devi yamune taap harini
Shri Vaye snatumichami jale sinsmidam kuru.

Meaning, come, O mother who removes our sorrows, we have come under your shelter, make us pure. You have to remember all these by heart, that is why I have spoken them in a singsong way, so that it is easy to remember these. Now, you have to wear your clothes. See, the clothes may not be expensive, but they must be clean. The clothes that you have worn today, you should not wear tomorrow. There is a mantra for wearing the clothes also. But, if I specify too many mantras, then you will not be able to do them. It may seem too much to you, but this is not too much. It is necessary. You spend one hour in performing your daily duties, so you should spend some time for this also. The one who gives us so much, we should thank him in this way. Do you not have this much time for him? You try doing all this and you will yourself experience how fragrant your life has become. This is the realisation of great men. Let us remember God in the end –

Satyanarayan narayan narayan,
surya narayan narayan narayan
Bhaj man narayan narayan narayan Shrimanarayan.....
Shri Dwarkadheesh ki jai, balkrishna lal ki jai
Sadgurudev ki jai, balkrishna lal ki jai
Sadgurudev ki jai, om namo parvati
pataye har har mahadev
Jai jai shri radhe-3 shri vrindavan bihari lal ki jai.

Meaning, say Satyanarayan, narayan, narayan surya narayan narayan narayan, Glory be to Dwarkadhessh, glory be to the infant God, Glory be to the noble guru, glory be to the infant God, Glory be to the noble guru, glory be to Shiva and Parvati, Glory be to Mahadev, glory be to Shri Radhe, Glory be to the one who lives in Vrindavan.

✻ CHAPTER 4 ✻

Shrimad Vallabhacharya says –

Agyaanat ath va gyaanat kritmatamnivedanam
Yae Krishna satkrit pranaestesham ka parivedana.

–Fourth couplet

God Shri Krishna is the incarnation of beauty and bliss. He is the creator of the world, he is ever pure, he is the one who provides shelter to the devotees. To surrender everything to this merciful and loving God, is service. In acharya Vallabhacharya's pure thought process, there is one action, and the fruit of that action is not different from the action. The fruit of all service is one. Whereas in the actions and worship that human beings do, the action is one, but the fruit of that action is different because there is a feeling of accomplishment. The action and fruit of the action of the great guru are only one and that is to make the ruler of the entire universe, God Shyamsunder (an epithet of Lord Krishna) happy and to serve him. It is said in Shandilya Sutras – The fruit of devotion to God is only devotion. The fruit of service is only service. The fruit of remembrance is only remembrance." Meaning, that the human souls do not do anything for their happiness. The singing of devotional songs is done to provide happiness to God.

"**Do devotion not for worldly happiness, but only for God.**"

The human beings are worried. This is the reason for Dave ji coming to the acharya. Maharaj, these worldly problems trouble me. It is possible that the human being has not surrendered fully. Here, the great guru is demonstrating 'shravan bhakti' in the fourth couplet.

There are three things in the fourth couplet. One is knowledge through which the human soul gained knowledge of what he was doing. How he was doing it? What will happen to me? This is a dedication of the best type. Dedication of medium type is that in which the human soul has dedicated itself according to the traditions, according to his family, or according to his community. He has dedicated himself without knowing what that supreme element is whom he is dedicating himself to. The third type of dedication is one in which the human soul has no knowledge of God nor what he is doing. For example, if someone has taken renuunciation during childhood and has dedicated himself during childhood, he does not have full knowledge of what he is doing. He is discussing these three types of dedication in this couplet.

The system of a disciple sitting at the feet of the guru and obtaining knowledge is called 'shruti (listening)'. The guru speaks and the disciple listens. This is 'shruti.' In the ancient times, the mind was so pure that the disciple used to grasp on listening for the first time. There was no need for paper. Today, in the fourth couplet, we are seeing the 'shruti' path only. How does the human soul receive mature knowledge? First of all, what is that element to which the human soul is dedicating itself? It is very important to have knowledge of this. Although the Vedas also say that what is the supreme element, even we don't have knowledge about that. This creates disappointement in the minds of people many times that when even the Vedas are unable to know what that supreme element is, then how can we unintelligent and powerless people know about it. See, "To know God, you don't need knowledge, but need the power to realise him." If there is love for God, then the seeker will have knowledge also, he will have devotion also, he will have action also, he will have dedication also. This is the supreme element, no one can say this. This is not possible. In our Gujarat, the people of one community keep a fast on the second of the month of Ashad. Till they do not see the moon on the night of the second, they do not eat food. The moon on the second is very small. If there are some old people in the family, then they may not be able to see this moon. If the children see it and say, "Come outside, the moon has risen." And if the old mothers come outside and are not able to see the moon, then they will ask the children, "Son, where is the moon?" So, if the son is an adult and intelligent, he will ask the mother, "Mother, are you able to see that mango tree?" The mother will say, "Yes, I am able to see that." Then he will ask, "Are you able to see the right branch of that tree?" Then the mother will say that she is able to see that also. Then, the son will ask, "Are you able to see that parrot sitting on the branch?" The mother will say that she is able to see that also. Then, the son will ask, "Are you able to see the moon that is in front of the beak of the parrot?" The mother looked approximately near that point and said, "Yes, yes, son. I am able to see the moon. Come, let us have our food." So, there is no relation between the mango tree, the beak of the parrot, and the moon that is situated in the sky thousands of miles away. But, the old mother is able to see that moon through the medium of these, and the intelligent son is able to show his mother the moon through the medium of this tree and the parrot. Similarly, the sages have done this to show God to unintelligent people like us. See in front of this Upanishad, these Vedas, and these mantras, God is sitting just above them. Otherwise, there is no relation of the Vedas, mantras, and the Upanishads with God. Only God himself knows himself completely. No one can say that God is like this. Yes, the devotees are able to experience something. But, if they are able to obtain full knowledge, then the devotee becomes one with God. Till one is aware of the body, till then the feeling of separation from God will remain. Till ego is there, one cannot experience God.

"The person who is immersed in worldly desires cannot experience God."

You will have to discard the worldly desires. If you keep fulfilling your senses, then you will not experience God. Till you find the fruits of the world sweet, till then you should understand that the journey has not started. The being is sleeping till then. The great men have hinted in the religious books that God is like this. And we have accepted that he is kind and merciful. Why is he like this? No one knows this. God has said in the Gita, "This Vyas, these 'devtaas' (celestial beings) don't know me. Listening and reading such words of the Gita, one feels how lonely this God is. There is nobody he can call his own. There is nobody who is equal to him –

"**Purush prasiddh prakash nidhi prakat...**"

Meaning, how lonely is my God. Imagine if you have to stay alone in a room for two hours, you become restless, whereas God is completely alone. There is nobody with Him. So, maybe he also wants that someone should call him son or brother, someone should love him. That is why he sometimes comes to be with Kaushalya, sometimes with Yashoda. Otherwise, why would God need to do all this drama? He is also hungry for love.

Gyaanat athva agyaanat ....ka parivedana.

The acharya is reminding again and again in this couplet – **ka parivedana**? **Ka parivedana**? Only that person will worry who does not believe in the capabilities of his God. We have heard that when the battle of the Mahabharat was taking place, then at the time of ceasefire during nightfall, the people of the opposing sides would meet and ask about each other's welfare. Then, the sinner Duryodhan used to make strategies for the next days' war along with Shakuni. Someone asked Arjun that why he did not make strategies for the next days' war like Duryodhan? Why did he go to sleep without any worry? Arjun gave only one reply –

"I sleep peacefully because Krishna is awake." So, when I believe in Krishna then why should I worry? My daughter is not yet married. The business is not running well. Why do you worry? This means that your faith is not strong. Yes, you may do worship, you may count the beads of the rosary, you may take the name of God, maybe thinking that if God is anywhere, he will help me. Then, your faith is not strong enough. When God gave a glimpse of his glory, he said that Arjun faith and belief are born in '**alolta**'. Then, Arjun asked, "What is **alolta**?" God said – "**Sthavaranam Himalaya.**" (meaning, stability like the Himalayas). When stability like the Himalayas comes into the human being, then faith is born. Tulsi Baba has written –

"Tehi karan himgiri upjai, janani parvati tanu pai"
Bhavani shankaro vando shradhha vishwas rupino
Yamyam binam na pashyanti"

Meaning, 'faith' which is like Parvati, is born, in 'complete stability' like the Himalayas. So, our journey has not started till now. Till now, we don't even have faith whether God exists or not. We think that if he is somewhere, he will be useful for us. This is not so. Who is running such a big creation? If the blood pressure or temperature of your body deviates even a little bit, you do not remain alive. So, who is holding these stars, these galaxies, this Sun? If this earth moves two steps closer to the Sun, then all the ice on the earth will melt. If it goes two feet away, then all of us will die of cold. Then, who controls all these? Science has not reached there till now and it can never reach till there. How strange is this creation! Who is the one who brings the clouds on time? Who is the one who brings the seasons on time?

Biban kaho kitna hansi, rangrej dekho kya hansi…

Meaning, it is surprising that in God's creation there is no repitition. No one face is like another. There is so much diversity. There is only one Vivekanand. There can be no other Vivekanand. He will be a little less or more than him. When we see all this, our mind stops working.

Khuda hai kharabi akal usme jyadi
Aadi anaadi ka karta kahaya
Kaun aag paani soon mitti miladi ek adam banaya
Ya naagpash dasham ka tamasha do kalma padaya
Muradam kahe jab sahi karke dekha
Jo khuda ne kiya vo akal mein na aya

Meaning, his drama is beyond our comprehension. So, why worry? You are irrational. He is rational. You are limited. He is unlimited. You are unknowledgable. He is knowledgable.

There was a gambler. He used to gamble. Once, he won some money in a game. So, he bought a very expensive necklace with that money. He went to give it to his lover. He was drunk, so he could not see the way. He fell in a ditch and he got wounded. He felt that now he would die, and that if he died someone else would take that necklace, and his lover would not get that necklace. So, at that time, using his intelligence, he offered that necklace to Krishna. He thought that if God was somewhere, he may be useful. Even otherwise, that necklace was going away from him. As soon as he offered the necklace to Krishna, he died. After death, when his soul was taken to Yamraj (God of Death), he said to Chitragupt, "See the details of his actions." Chitragupt said, " Maharaj, he has not done any good deed. All his deeds were bad. He will go straight to hell." Yamraj said, "See carefully, he must have done something good." When Chitragupt saw again, he said, "Yes, Maharaj, on the last page it is written that at the time of dying, he offered an expensive necklace to Krishna." Then, Yamraj said, "He has done a very good deed. In return for this, he will get the throne of heaven for two seconds, and in return for the other deeds, he will have to stay in hell." Then, that soul was asked, "Will you go to heaven first or hell?" He said, "Maharaj, first let me see heaven for two seconds and sit on the throne of Indra, then I will go to hell." Yamraj said, "Okay, even though unknowingly, you have done a good deed, so you have received the right to sit for two seconds on the throne of Indra." As soon as that soul sat on the throne, then Narad ji saw him and came towards him saying Narayan, narayan, narayan and laughed. The soul asked him, "Narad ji, why do you laugh?" Narad ji said, "See, you unknowingly offered a necklace to Krishna, so you got two seconds in heaven. If the human beings offer all their actions to Krishna, then what will the result of that be? Just think." The soul said, "Then, is all this mine." Yamraj said; "Yes, all this is yours, but only for two seconds." So, that soul said, "Okay, if it is for two seconds, then so be it." He said, "Call brahmins and pandits." When the Brahmins and pandits came, he said, "Get Airavat elephant." When that elephant was brought, he offered it to Krishna. Then, he called for all the beautiful women of heaven and offered them to Krishna, then he called for all the jewels of heaven and offered those to Krishna. Then, he offered the throne of Indra to Krishna, then he offered the Kalpvriksh (wishing tree) to Krishna. When two seconds passed, Indra came and saw that everything had been offered to Lord Krishna, he asked, "Who has done all this?" He got the reply that this was done by that human soul who had got the throne for two seconds. That soul was then told, "Come, your time has finished. Now, you will go to hell." When he was being taken to hell, Narad ji came and said, "Yamraj, what sort of justice is this? When he unknowingly offered a necklace to Krishna, you gave him the throne of Indra for two seconds. Now, when he has knowingly offered everything to Krishna, then how can you give him hell? Now, he will become Indra. Now, he cannot go to hell. Then, Yamraj asked, "What should we do with him?" Narad said, "Send him to earth. On the earth, it was the rule of Virochan at that time who was a descendant of Prahlad. He did not have any child. History says that when Virochan did a yagna to pray for a child, then God said that he would have a son like Indra. So, when Virochan had a son, it was the same human soul that sat on the throne for two seconds and gave the whole of heaven to Krishna. This same Baliraja was Virochan's son. This is Baliraja's history. When he has given charity knowingly, then God is staying there till today and protecting him, and in the future will give him the throne of Indra. So, it is said –

Agyanaat va gyaanat...

Meaning, when you have dedicated yourself knowingly or unknowingly, then why worry? Only the knowledgable will achieve God, it is not so. Otherwise, what will happen to people like us?

Na tapobhin na vedashch na gyanen naapi karmana
Haririsadhyate sadhyate bhavtaya pramanam tatr gopika

Meaning, you can't achieve God by meditation. You can't

achieve God by undertaking Vedic rituals. "**Hari sadhyate bhaktaya.**" Meaning, God is achieved by devotion. Like the gopikas achieved God. God's speech is a proof. God told Durvasa, "**Aham bhakt paradhino**," meaning I am ruled by the desire of my devotees. Could God not have said that he was ruled by knowledge, or that he was ruled by meditation? He said he was ruled by his devotees. He was ruled by love. He was not ruled by the orthodox traditions.

Mahara re bandhya vaishnav chode
vaishnav bandhya main na chutu re
Ek baar jo vaishnav bandhyen bandhan
te nav chutyo re...

See, don't derive your own meaning from our words. Understand the meanings of our sentences. We are not saying that you will not achieve him by meditation, or that you will not achieve him by knowledge, or by rituals. Otherwise, in this 'kaliyug' how many people are there who have achieved enlightenment, how many people are there whose renunciation has strengthened? Tell me. You come to listen to the discourse in the tent and you bring your slippers with yourself. You can't leave a pair of slippers, how will you leave the world. Maharaj, knowledge and renunciation are very difficult. How many people can do it?

Gyan ke panth kripan ki dhara...

Meaning, in traditional rituals, a great deal of purity is needed. Today, it is not possible to gather the pure materials. How many people are there who can do a pure pronunciation. So, the acharya is not saying that you cannot get him by meditation, knowledge, or traditional rituals. But, he is trying to say that today in the 'kaliyug' the ease with which one can achieve God by walking on the path of devotion, it is not possible to achieve him as easily by any other way.

Hari sadhyate bhaktaya – For devotion, you need great love. The peak of love is devotion – "**Sa param prem rupa.**" Narad ji is saying, "How is this God who is like the nectar of immortality?" In Bhakti Sutra, Narad has said this that the person in whose life he comes, his life becomes likes nectar. In the path of devotion, God lifts the entire responsibility of the devotee on his shoulders. Responsibility means worry, what else? So, take the pure meaning here, don't take the wrong meaning. Service means to provide happiness and satisfaction to God. And happiness and satisfaction, you can provide yourself only, no one else can do it. So, worship him yourself. These gopis did not close their nostrils and sit down. These gopis did not do '**swaha, swaha**' (worship ritual) anywhere. Knowledge will come into your hearts itself when there is devotion. **The meaning of devotion is that it is the mother of good qualities, and the meaning of attachment is that it is the mother of all bad qualities.** It is not sure whether the knowledgeable great man has devotion or not, whether he has renunciation or not. But, the devotee will have knowledge and renunciation everything. Tulsi baba has said –

Bhardwaj muni bas hi pryaga tin hi ram pad ati anuraga
Tapas sam dam daya nidhana paramarath
path param sujana.

Those who have love for God, that is devotional love, then knowledge, power, mercy everything come to him themselves.

Agyaanat athva gyaanat atam nivedanam. Meaning, whether you do it knowingly or unknowingly, but dedicate yourself to him. Dave ji, a relation with God is formed in three ways - Excellent, medium, and poor. **Agyaanat** meaning a relation with God borne out of ignorance. Some people say that we had gone to a guru and had taken initiation as a disciple in the childhood. Now, our guru is no more and we have forgotten all the rules, so you please initiate us again. It is not this way. You were ignorant at that time. But, the person who initiated you was knowledgeable. You catch hold of that mantra. If you have forgotten the rules, then you can ask. There is no need for initiation as someone's disciple again. There is nothing to worry.

There has been a Sadanand Maharaj in our Vrindavan. It

was his daily ritual that he would come out of his hut everyday to Banke Bihari to catch a glimpse of God. Chaube ji of that place used to see that this is a blind person and he comes everyday to see God. One day, it was raining. Our Lord Krishna is in the Kunj lane of Vrindavan. In the dark, if your feet slip then you can fall. The priest said to him, "Maharaj, if you come to see God in the summer or winter season, then it is okay. In this rainy season, you may fall and hurt yourself. Then, you are not able to see also. You see by the eyes of the mind. So you can see God in your hut also." Sadanand ji said, "Yes, brother, I am blind. But I come here because my God can see me. My God is not blind! He sees me daily. So, I come here in the rainy season also."

So, the acharya is saying here that even though you had taken initiation as a child and you were ignorant; but, God knows everything. He knows that this human being had formed a relation with me. So, even though you did it in ignorance – why worry? God will worry about you Himself. Like when the potter first brings mud, he sifts through it. Then he makes a utensil of it. Tell God that there are countless faults in me, you please forgive me. O God! You are capable of doing anything –

"Kamadi dosh rahitam mein kuru."

Meaning, please make me a clean and pure person so that I am able to serve you. God can do it. Why do you worry? This is a relation of the third type.

The second is the relation of the medium type – when you took initiation, you did not have complete knowledge. You thought everyone is taking initiation, I will also take. I should have a guru. But, you have the knowledge of what you are doing. But, you don't have full faith on God. You take initiation seeing other people doing the same. This is the second type.

The third type is the initiation of the excellent type. In this, the relation with God is formed knowingly. The person who is forming the relation is fully aware of what he is doing. He has full faith in God, and he also has full faith in his guru. He knows that his guru is able, he will help him swim across the sea of emotion. So, always pray in life that you get such a guru who is able to help you swim across the ocean of ignorance and nescience. Because the sage who is able, he himself also swims across and the one who comes close to him, also swims across –

'Sa tarti, sa tarti, sa lokans-taaryati.'

(Narad Bhakti Sutra)

Meaning, he will himself swim across and he will help you also to swim across. So, call out daily –

"Mile koi aisa sant fakir
Pahuncha de bhav dariya ke teer.
Taat mile, puni maat mile, such bhraat mile,
juvati sukhdai
Raj mile, gajraj mile, sab saaj mile man vanchit bhai.
Lok mile parlok mile vaikunth mile man vanchit bhai
Durlabh bhai, sant samagam durlabh bhai,
sant samagam durlabh bhai."

Meaning, may I find such a guru who helps me to cross this sea of ignorance.

The soul knows who he is and in whose shelter he is going. The acharya has said that it is possible that in this age you are not able to find a good guru. Because the soul is ignorant, how can it find out that this is a good guru? Till now there was the tradition of taking a little child to the guru and having him initiated as a disciple. But, our advice is that don't take it as a principle. If your faith arises on a great man, then first question him, have curiosity, examine him. To make a person a guru is a question of life and death. If he is a good guru, he will give an answer according to the scriptures. "**To make someone a disciple is easy, to retain him as a disciple is difficult.**" Many people say that we took initiation as a disciple from this guru, but now we are not happy with him. Please initiate us as your disciple. I tell them, no, it is not possible for me to initiate you again. You take initiation as someone's disciple once in your life. Yes, I can definitely give you knowledge. If you did not examine him before, then nothing can be done now.

A true guru 'Sadguru' is one after going into whose shelter, your doubts are resolved, who takes away your emotional turmoils, whose nearness gives you peace, in whose mind there is always this worry that how will my disciple gain realisation? Otherwise, the gurus of today are –

"**Lobhi guru lalchi chela, donon ka narak me thelam thela.**" Meaning, the greedy guru and the greedy disciple, both belong to hell.

Kabir has said –

Janta boojhta nahin anboojh kiya nahin koi
Andhe ko andha mila raah bataave koi.

Meaning, one who has a narrow outlook can never be a guru. The one who is fixed on his own beliefs, the one who has a negative outlook can never be a guru. The work of a good guru is not to break and demolish, the work of a guru is to make the faith of his disciple mature, not to break it. Karpatri ji Maharaj used to say "**Agyaanat va gyaanat**....anyone who has achieved oneness with God whether it is with an excellent, medium, or poor type of relation, then that person has nothing to worry. See, in the '**pushthi**' path of devotion, the main thing is service. As far as our opinion is concerned, service should be done with the soul instead of through actions. If the body does some action, but the mind is not concentrated on it, then what is the use? If you do not believe us, then the proof of this is the gopikas. The gopikas have done the service with their heart. That is why they have been able to achieve God.

"**Shri Krishan poojyate bhaktaya.**"

Meaning, the guru orders that the devotee has to do the service himself. There should be no hesitation in this. See, in "**Do sau bavan vaishnavan ki vaarta**" (name of a book) there was a devotee Damodar Das. He was from a very happy and wealthy family. He used to fill a pot of water from the Yamuna and bring it himself to serve the Lord. One day, his father-in-law saw this and he did not like it. So, he said to Damodar Das, "Why don't you ask some servant to bring the water?" When the servant brings the water, you serve the Lord. Damodar Das kept quiet. The next day he told his wife, "Come, today we both will go to bring the water of the Yamuna." The wife was obedient. She put the pot on her head and started walking with him. The father-in-law saw that today his daughter was also with him. The father-in-law understood his mistake. He understood what was service.

The acharya has said that if you want to do service, then look at Ambrish, see Damodar Das. Surdas has said – **Sur bhajan kali keval kije**. Meaning, do devotion yourself, sing devotional songs yourself, do service yourself. Do it with your body, wealth, and heart. Don't borrow from anyone. There is a story of a Shri Nandini in this same '**Do sau bavan vaishnav vaarta**' She was poor, so she would keep only a little bit of sugar for God as an offering. One day, she thought that God would not be happy with this little offering, so she borrowed money from a relative of hers. From that money, she offered a 56-course meal to God. But, God refused to accept that. He said that he would not accept that offering because she had borrowed the money from someone. He said that her little bit of sugar and basil leaves were dear to him, and that he would not take this offering which was bought with someone else's money. I want to tell this to the new generation especially. A science is attached to every aspect of worship. If you go to bathe, you should never bathe naked. By doing this, you commit a crime against the God of Water (Varun Dev). After bathing, you should start washing from the top, not from the bottom. If you have wiped till the hips, don't bring the towel back upwards again. It has become impure. Even if your clothes are old, they should be pure and clean. Wash your own clothes yourself. Don't let anyone else touch your clothes. While bathing, invoke all rivers. Keep chanting the mantra that your guru gave you. After becoming pure after taking the bath, take holy water of the Brij land with the feeling that God resides in Yamuna river. God is taking his daily walk there. God is grazing cows in Brij even today. Some people who are deserving are able to see God there today also.

"**Atati yad bhavaan chaaryan pashun, nalin sundaram naath te padam.**"

Meaning, the soil of Brij has been sanctified by the touch of the Lord's lotus-feet. This is a form of the river Yamuna. The people of Brij still believe that till you have not rolled in the soil of Raman-Reti, your journey to Brij is incomplete. So, by drinking this air of Brij, you get the right to utter the name of God. By putting it on your eyes, you get the right to see God. While taking the air of Brij as 'charnamrit' (holy water) recite this mantra –

"Grihnami gokuladhish charnamrit madrad
Atstavatah seva na siddhye mayi dine dayam kurum."

Meaning, when you drank it, you got the right to recite the name of God. When you put it in your eyes, you get the right to see God. When you put it in your mouth, you get the right to take God's name, and when you touch it to your ear, then you get the right to hear God's name.

"Hari om bhadrakarne vishwayubhyam devah."

Meaning, O God, may your name come into my ears from the four corners. Then, touch the holy water to your heart region and say, "God, come and live in my heart." Remember, that this is not only the holy water from the lotus feet of God, this is a symbol of the river Yamuna, secondly, this is a symbol of God, thirdly, it is a symbol of the men of God, of the gopis. So, Yamuna ji came into our pot, God came and the great man Vallabhacharya came. Our pot, means this heart, this body...

Mahara ghat ma virajata srinath ji
Jamuna ji mahara prabhu...

See, whenever you perform some action related to worship, there should be a towel and a pot of water in your hand always. It is necessary to wash your hands after every action for purity and cleanliness. After rinsing the mouth, you have to do 'tilak' (putting a dot on the forehead as a mark of prayer). Every community has their own traditions regarding 'tilak'. Why do we do tilak? Patanjali has especially emphasized on the 'Ingla and Pingla' (two veins of the body). These two veins go from the 'mooladhar chakra' (one of the six ganglions of the body according to Hatha Yoga) across the back to the brain till the 'brahm randhra' (suture on the top of the head). Between these two is a thin vein, Sushumana. The source of energy, i.e. the power to awaken 'kundalini (one of the prominent ganglions of the body according to Hatha Yoga)' is situated in the 'mooladhar'. When we concentrate from the 'mooladhar' for thinking, meditation, and for concentration, then energy is produced. When a machine works for some time, then due to energy produced, it becomes hot in a little while, and arrangements for cooling it are made by water and air. Similarly, so that the mind does not heat up too much due to the heat produced by meditating, and there is no disease caused in the mind, so a 'tilak' is put in the centre of the concentration point i.e. the 'agya chakra'. Otherwise, the devotee may suffer from anger or other problems. In the 'tilak' there is usually 'roli' (powder produced from mixture of turmeric and lime), 'chandan' (sandalwood), which provides coolness. Like previously, people used to anoint mud to the utensils of mud at the time of cooking, so that they would not break. So, Maharaj, so that your brain does not burst because of the sins, heat, and suffering of this world, we put a 'tilak' on the forehead. Thirdly, this 'tilak' is a symbol of the feet of God. God had kept his feet on the 'kaliya naag' (black serpent). Even today, this sign is found on the foreheads of the snakes.

Kusumit kanan ranchit prabhu mand hasit vadanam
Fanivar kaliya daman yakshswar vahanam

So, by doing 'tilak' even your migraine can become better. While doing 'tilak' recite the following mantra –

Dandakar lalate syad padmakaram tu vakshasi
Lalate keshav vigyanam, narayanam vakodare
Vakshsthale madhavach govind kanth koopke
Shirdharam vambaho padmanaam tu pristath
Sande damodaram vidyam vasudev ch murdhani.

Now, we have become ready for service. Now, see the secret of service. When you will open the door of the temple, i.e. the house of Krishna, then first of all take permission from the person whose disciple you are about how you should do the service.

Remember, without taking permission, you cannot enter. So, first come and sit on the door and awaken God. There is a tradition for awakening God also. You can recite couplets or you can sing songs –

Jago bansi vaare lalna jago more laal re
Rajni biti bhor bhayo hai ji, ji, ji
Ghar ghar khule kivade ji, ji, ji
Gopi dahi mathat suniyat kangan jhankare ji
Jago bansi vaare lalna...
Utho lal ji bhor bhayo hai ji, ji, ji
Suno re gwale thaade dwar re ji
Gwal sab karat kulahal jai jai shabd pukare ji
Jaago bansi vaare...
Makhan roti haath mein linhi ji, gauvan ke rakhware ji
Jaago bansi vare...

See, there is a procedure of installing the idol of God in the temple also. First of all, according to your capacity, make a four-cornered stool. It can be of silver, of sandalwood, whatever your capability may be. Then, spread a clean white cloth on it. It can be of silk also. Make a good pillow. Two on the right side, two on the left side, one below. The pillow should be of cotton, not of fibre. God likes natural things only. Otherwise, according to Bhagwat, today he is decorated with the splendour of the forests. How does God look –

Varhapidam natwar vapu karanyo karnikaram
Vibhadra vasah kanakpisham vaijayanti ch malam.
Randhran venoradharsudhya puryan gopvrindeh
Vrindaranyam swapadramanam pravishad geet kirtih.
Shri Krishna Govind Hare Murari,
he naath narayan vasudev.

So, to install the idol of God, lay a bed, or a cradle, or a palanquin, as is your capability. Decorate it. When you enter the room for service, recite this mantra

Bhagwadwanı bhagwan namaste dal karomitat
Abhi kuruhayarthey padosarpanam

Now, after entering the temple, first of all, you have to clean it. So, first of all sweep the room. The broom should be of a clean cloth or of a peacock's feathers. If it is big temple, anoint it with the dung of the cow. If it is of marble, clean it with a clean wet cloth and then with a dry cloth. Keep chanting this couplet-

Marjanat Krishna grihasaya manovikshep man rajah
Nashneti tadarthantu marjayami tathastu te.
Atamano gyan upasaya duritasya kshayalahi
Karomi lokovalayo ka tadgrihe gokuleshwarah.

What is the thought behind the sweeping? "**Mano-vikshepamraj**" meaning, whatever dust has come in my mind, whatever mental turmoils are in my mind; O God! clean this dust from this mind because you have to reside in this temple of my mind. What did Prahlad ji say –

"Kamadi dosh rahitam kuru manasam ch."

Meaning, Maharaj, remove this shortcoming of mine and what I want from you is-

Bhaktim prayach raghupungav nirbharam mein

Meaning, O God! Give me your pure devotion. Salute God in the morning and say –

He Gokulesh! Kamal nabhaya tubhayam namami.
He Lakshmi kantaya tubhayam namami.
He garud dhwajaye tubhayam namami.
He kamal netraye tubhayam namami.
He bhakt vatsalaya tubhayam namami
He shantakaraya tubhayam namami

While sweeping, all these thoughts should be in your mind. Then, God will ask – What do you want so early in the morning? Then say, "**Maharaj, kamadi dosh rahitam kuru manasam ch.**" meaning "God free me of greed, lust and other shortcomings." "What else do you want?" Say, "**Bhaktim prayach**." meaning "devotion". What else do you want? "Nothing else, Maharaj. I speak the truth nothing else. See, there is a special relation of God with the colour white. Brahma ji sits on a white lotus. The mountains where Lord Shiva dwells, the Kailash, is draped with white snow. And God himself dwells in the sea, which is of white colour. White means pure, gentle, peaceful. So, our mind should also be like this. While doing service, if you are not able to do this, then atleast chant the eight-lettered mantra.

Now, when you install God on the throne or the cradle, then keep two pillows on the right and left side, one behind the back. There should be a pillow beneath the feet. The comfort should be as if God is sleeping in the lap of mother Yashoda. The pillows on the left and right hand side are the arms of mother Yashoda. Now, we will keep water in the 'jhaari' (small pitcher in which water used for worship is kept). The jhaari ji is a symbol of Yamuna ji. In the morning, when you empty the jhaari ji, don't throw away the water, drink it because God must have drunk that water. That water is equal to the nectar of immortality (amrit). Remember Yamuna ji at the time of drinking-

Dhan shri yamune kripa karo shri gokul brij such aap jo
Tam mota cho ji maharani tam jeevtani karuna jaani
Hamne sharane le ja taari dhan shri yamune....
Shri vrindavan nighat man nahaoon,
brij ni raj mein ahnirsh yamune
Ji nat rito taap jo, dhan shri yamune....
Shri gokul yamuna ji galiyo ma maharaj mujhne tyamadiya
Mahara sakal manorath safaltaya dhan shri yamune...
Chalo to thahiye brijvaasi, parikrama kariye chaurasi
Mahari janam maran ni kati faansi dhan shri yamune....
Shri giriraj dharan ki jai

✻ CHAPTER 5 ✻

Shri Vallabhacharya says –

**"Tatha nivedane chinta tyajaya shri purushotame.
Viniyogeapi sa tyajaya samrtho hi hari swatah."**

–Fifth couplet

This is how the difference between the soul and the physical has been described in the scriptures. The physical is faulty, changeable, limited and is tied by the boundaries of time. The soul is limitless, faultless, eternal, all-knowing, and unchanging. There are four kinds of calamities which have been described in the scriptures. Among these, one is momentary calamity. This world changes every minute. Every minute, there is a calamity happening here. On one side there is creation, and on the other side, there is annihilation. The body is a symbol of the physical. The man is the soul, and nature is the physical. Man is unbreakable, unchangeable. He remains the same in all the three ages. The one who is breakable can be divided, can be measured. In this fifth couplet, the acharya has made us realise the omnipresence and indivisibility of God and called God the best among all men. Nature and men are different. God is the supreme soul, whereas nature is a physical thing. This body of ours, if it is here today, then it is not in Delhi. This is being limited by physical boundaries. God is here also and there also. He is everywhere, he is always there, and he is equal for all. Our limits are some five feet, sixty kilograms, or five and a half feet and seventy kilograms. God is limitless.

It is the time of morning. The acharya is sitting. In front of him, Dave ji is sitting and there is worry on his face. Worry is of many types. Worry about wealth, worry about health, worry about the future. The one who is worried, how will he sit in meditation? How will he sing devotional songs? It is forbidden in the scriptures to sing devotional songs with an upset mind. The great men say that you should not meditate with an upset mind. It will not be fruitful. You may do it for a short time, but do it peacefully. Your mind should concentrate on God, this is service. Love for God is service, is devotion.

Worry troubles not only the worldly people, but the sages also these days. They have to run the cowshed, they have to get a hospital constructed. They have to run the ashram. They have the responsibility of their disciples also. If the great men has not attained wisdom till now, if his renunciation has not become strengthened, then he may worry. If their faith in God is not complete, then even after becoming gurus, the great men can be worried. Otherwise think that what my God is doing, how he is doing, it is appropriate. The meaning of dedication is to surrender everything. When I don't have anything, then why should I worry about anything. Till the feeling of 'I am' is there, till the feeling, "This is mine" is there, till then there is worry. "I don't have the wisdom. God has the wisdom, what he does will be correct." Keep this feeling. Ego and attachment, due to this reason not only the human beings, but the 'devtaas' (celestial beings) also worry. At the time of the Mahabharat war, Indra got worried that the son of the Sun, Karan, had an impassable armour and divine earrings, then how would Arjun, who is a part of me, be able to win over him. So, even the 'devtaas' become worried due to this feeling of 'mine'. It is difficult for human beings to rise above 'mine' but not impossible. If you try, then you will definitely be successful. Do it today. Tomorrow will be too late.

'**During adversity, wait for the opportunity; and during good times, utilise the opportunity.**' During adversity, the capability of a human being is recognised. During adversity, strength is generated. God has given even the smallest of living beings the wisdom to deal with adversity. The human beings of today start crying with even a little bit of adversity. This thing of mine was destroyed. When nothing belonged to you, then how could it be destroyed? The lyricist has said –

You are getting worried needlessly,
you are spending your life needlessly.
The human soul is immortal,
you are living your life in fear needlessly.
Whatever has happened was good,
whatever is happening is good.
Whatever will happen will be good, this union is true.
Forget about yesterday. Why are you crying today.
You are getting worried needlessly....

The guru is sitting in the front. See, when Arjun asked Krishna the question that what is a dedicated person like? How does he speak? How does he eat? How does he behave? God said, "Arjun, a dedicated person does not behave differently from others." Only his way of doing things is different. A dedicated person remains calm. Vallabhacharya ji always remains happy, and the human being in front is in a worried state. In the fifth couplet, this worry has come that I have surrendered everything, but has God accepted my surrender? I don't have any proof by which I can understand whether God has accepted my surrender.

"Tatha nivedene chinta tyajaya shri purushotame.
Viniyoapi sa tyajaya samartho hi harih swatah." (5)

Meaning, gurudev, after dedicating ourselves, we get busy in worldly works. So, when we have offered our powers and senses to God, then how can we use them in worldly tasks? Utilising this body in worldly duties is not a crime, is it?

See, Krishna is sitting on Arjun's chariot as a charioteer. In one hand, he has the whip and in the other hand he has the reigns of the horses. He is happy. When Arjun has handed over the chariot to Lord Krishna, then he did not worry that where will my chariot go now? What is the reason for this? Arjun knows that his God is capable. "**Samartho hi hari,**" (God is capable) the Upanishads say. Human beings have handed over the reigns of this body to the brain. The person who trusts his brain on this path, is never successful. The brain does not know where the welfare of the human soul lies. Our selfishness changes every moment. Sometimes we are attracted towards our wife, sometimes towards money, sometimes prestige, sometimes entertainment. The mind is never stable.

See, when the arrow is shot, its direction is straight. It does not waver. That is why it goes straight to its destination. Because it know its target. Human beings do not have the knowledge of their target. If a human being becomes determined that yes I want this thing only, then his welfare is definite. If the waves of indecision are not quietened, then the nature will not become stable. If the nature is unstable, then the mind will not be stable. If the mind is not stable, then meditation is not possible.

The acharya is knowledgeable. In this couplet, he has used two words '**Purushottam**' (best among all men) and '**hari.**' What is the meaning of **purushottam**? The acharya has used this term after deep thought. Otherwise, God has thousands of names.

Hari tharo hai hazaar naam ki kari kankotari
Roj-roj badle mukam kya naam rakh ri kankotari
Mathura ma mohan tu gokul mein gwadio-2
Dwarika na rai ran chod kya naam rakh ri kankotari...
Hari tharo...
Koi sita ram kahe koi radhe shyam-2
Koi kahe nand no kishore kya naam rakh ri kankotari
Hari tharo hai...

Meaning, God, you have many names. So, two names have come – one "Purushottam" and one "Hari". Acharya is using the word with the desire to remove the worry from the human beings' mind. In 'Vishnu Sahastranaam', there are 1000 names of God. Sitting in the jail, Acharya Vinoba Bhave wrote a very beautiful explanation of these. How can we explain 'Purushottam'? God himself said, "Listen, human being, why my name is Purushottam?"

Prathamakshar ateet aham aksharatapi chaintam
Atah asminloke vede chaham ateet purushottamah.

Meaning, I am indestructible, that is why people and the Vedas call me Purushottam. I am eternal. I am always present, I am equal. No one has been able to know me completely. Yes, they can definitely guess at my true nature. O human being, this is my sign. I am neither destructible, nor am I changeable. According to the time and place, I take on different forms. Sometimes, a man of action, sometimes a man of religion. Sometimes, I take a partial incarnation, sometimes I take a full incarnation on this earth. But, my basic qualities never change, and those who doubt this form of mine, what happens to them. Sati Maharani doubted me, she had to leave her body. Arjun had started to doubt, but God cautioned him – Arjun, '**Natr sanshaya.**' Arjun, don't doubt. That is why, I have been hailed in the Vedas.

The second name is 'Hari' which the guru has used. Whom do we call 'Hari'. There are many meanings of 'Hari' in Sanskrit. There is no living thing in this world which is not suffering from material, or divine, or intellectual pain. From a mosquito to Lord Brahma, nobody has been spared of this pain. Brahma ji is also worried about getting old and his job. Once, Brahma ji felt proud that if he were not there, then who would have created this world. I am the creator, and Lord Vishnu has become the Lord of this universe. He sleeps peacefully in the ocean. He went to God and said, "God, I am tired. Now, please release me from this work." God stood up, "Oh Brahmdev, what are you saying. How will we manage without you? Who will create this universe?" Brahma said, "No, God, now I cannot do this. Now, please release me." So, God said to Narad ji, "Okay, take Brahmdev's resignation letter." When Brahma was going away after handing in his resignation, in the front on the road where he was going, 1,000 Brahmas were coming sitting on 1,000 camels. They were exactly like him, one Brahma on each camel. Brahma ji was surprised. He asked them who they were. I have not created you. All those Brahmas spoke unanimously, "We are those who had taken leave from God from performing our work due to our pride. Today, we learnt that the present Brahma is also taking leave from his work. So, we are going to take his place." Then, Brahma ji realised his mistake and immediately asked for forgiveness from God. He took over his work again. So, here Lord Brahma is also worried. Our gopis say–

"Tav kathamritam tapt jeevanam
kavibhiriditam kalmshapaham
Shravan mangalam shrimadanatam bhuvi
grunanti te bhurida janah."

(From Gopi Geet)

"**Patang ghaur kiraneh dahyanti.**" Meaning, this world is burning in three kinds of fire. If at that moment someone remembers You, You take away (haran) all his three types of pain immediately. That is why you are Hari."

So, till you don't have faith on the name and form of God, till then you won't be able to generate love for God. God is very beautiful. We have read in the scriptures that when Shiva, Brahma etc. gods used to go to see God, then the light of God's '**sudarshan chakra**' (a discuss-like weapon) was so strong that they could not see God's face. They would just bow their heads in God's feet and come back.

When Tulsi baba set about to describe God's beauty, he said that he was like the Sun, the Moon, like lotus. Then, he said, no-no, he is like no one else. There is no one else like him, how can I compare him with anyone.

When Shankaracharya defined mother, he said that honey, grape, kheer are all sweet, but the speech cannot describe them. Because these substances are experienced by the tongue, and God is seen by the sight. He is a thing to experience. Those who have seen him had to say –

Ae shri aao te rang mane seed laga le
Ae mahari jaagi purab ni preet vithhala
Aao the rang mane seed laga le...
Ae das vaishnav ne asro tamaro vithhala
Ae mane karvi samarpan preet vithhala
Aao te rang...

"**Rasatama iti purushotamah.**" Meaning, God is like nectar. God is like love. God is the embodiment of mercy. He removes the three kinds of pain. That is why his name is Hari.

In the fifth couplet, the guru is explaining this only. O human being, God is capable. But, this does not mean that he will do all your worldly tasks. The meaning of capable is also that God knows all the qualities of a human soul. The human being has many defects. The extent of the faults depends on a person's nature and upbringing.

In this world, there is no one who is completely good. There is no one who is completely bad. The intensity of faults depends on the company, upbringing, and nature. So, the meaning of 'Hari samarth' is that God knows a human being is wicked from birth. He becomes worried at a little problem. Sugreev listened to the religious discourse till there were problems in his life. He had the company of a good guru like Hanuman. As soon as Hanuman ji's company stopped and he got a little favourable circumstances in his life, he became greedy and lustful. As soon as he got wealth, he became greedy –

Nari nayan jehi sar nahin laagaa...

Till he did not get the rule of the kingdom, everything was okay. But, as soon as he got it, all his faults came to the front. When his desire was not fulfilled, he felt angry also. So, the meaning of 'Hari samarth' is that God knows the good qualities and shortcomings of the human beings fully well.

Viniyogeyapi sa tyajaya...

The guru is saying that God knows that even after dedicating himself, he will wander elsewhere. So, God will remove your faults himself. You don't worry, O human being. Many times people ask me that at the time of worship and prayer, this thing happened, did it cause impurity? We have committed a crime, have we? No, God will free you from sin Himself. See, in 'Goverdhan Leela' these people used to worship Indra, God Himself told them that they should worship Annakoot. He showed them the correct path Himself. So, human being, you don't worry.

He will make everything all right. But, this also does not mean that you have got a licence to make mistakes. One mistake is committed intentionally, and one is by mistake. The one who commits it knowingly has to bear the punishment, but the one who commits it unknowingly does not have to. Valmiki was ignorant. When Narad ji gave him knowledge, then he realised. In the fourth para 'Moksh Prakaran' in the Shrimadbhagwat, this has been illustrated by the means of the story of the king who sacrificed animals during worship. It was said that the way the king was sacrificing animals for the worship, those animals would trouble him in the same way after his death. So, these sins that are done unknowingly are forgiven. But, if you take bribe knowingly, then it is unforgivable.

God is saying here that O human being! You don't worry about your inability. God is capable. He will free you from your sins. You only surrender before God. Appeal to God daily that O God, if you want that I should not commit sins, then you give me good sense. Before sleeping everyday, pray. Teach children to offer water to the Sun everyday. It is equal to theft to study without offering water to the Sun. The knowledge that is stolen cannot be successful. Eklavya and Karan had obtained knowledge by stealth, so they had to bear its punishment. At the time of sleeping, thank God. God, with your power, today I fulfilled my worldly duties. Now, you take your power back. Give it to me again in the morning. It is the mother's duty to give good values to the children. To only give him wealth is equal to doing enmity with a child. Shivaji was made Shivaji by his mother Jijabai. The mother who not only gives food, but also values, that mother is called a goddess. **Matr devo bhav, pitr devo bhav**. Meaning, the mother and father are like Gods.

"Don't sing praises of great men,
imbibe their good qualities."

"Do devotion for God, not for the result."

In the '**Garbhopanishad**' it has been said that while a child is in the womb, his age and destiny are written. So, don't try to achieve luxuries. Try to achieve God. That is not written in your fate. Whether it is 'sadhan bhakti' (devotion through resources) or any other type of devotion, do everything for God. In Navdha Bhakti, the human being is independent in seven types of devotion. In the other two, he is dependent. These cannot be done without the order of God. One is 'sakhya bhakti' (friendly devotion) and the other is 'paad seva' (serving the feet). Till God does not say, one cannot do 'paad seva'. When God gives the boatman the order – "**Devi aani jal paad pakharo, hot vilamb utarhi paro,**" then the boatman says –"**Ati anand umang anuraga charan saroj pakharan laga.**" So, 'shravan' (hearing), kirtan (singing devotional songs), smaran (rememberrance), vandan (bowing before someone), dasya (serving), pujan (worship), atamnivedan (dedicating oneself) are all independent types of devotion. In the other two, the human being is dependant. All these are 'sadhan bhakti.' The fruit of devotion is the devotion only. God, shravan, kirtan, whatever I am doing, I don't want to get anything out of that. The fruit of devotion is the devotion only.

In the words of Vritasur

Aham hare tab padaek mulam dasanudaso
bhavitasmi bhuyam
Manahsmareta supate gurnaste vaakkarm karoti kaay
Na naak pristham na parmeesthyam na
saarvmausam na rasadhipatyam
Na yog siddhi punarbhav vam samanjas
twam virhayay kankshe."

–*Shrimadbhagwad*

So, say daily –

Ram raghav, Ram raghav, Ram raghav, trahimam.
Krishna keshav Krishna keshav
Krishna keshav pahimaam.

From the nine types of devotion, a human being is free in seven types, and is dependent in the other two types. The last type of devotion is self-dedication. This is a little bit difficult. Here also the word dedication has come. The great guru is also saying this – **Tathapi nivedan chinta...**

Till ego and attachment don't go away, till then self-dedication is not possible. This world is incomplete. So, whenever we get anything, we get incomplete. God is complete. So, whenever we get Him, we get Him completely. So, you also have to dedicate yourself fully. Some people make a rule that they will get up at this time in the morning and do worship and then they will do Vedic rites. The devotion of such people does not progress. Some people are worshipping since twenty years, but they are still where they were before. This is suspended devotion. This is not progressive. The worship of Satya Narayan is not done on a particular day. The meaning of discourse is that the life should become true. If only the priest comes and chants the discourse, then nothing will happen out of that. Every moment of your life becomes true, this is discourse. Gandhi ji used to say that if truth comes into life and the name of Ram on the lips, then this ocean of ignorance and suffering could be crossed without a ship. This is not impossible, but, it is difficult. If a human being wants, he can do anything.

Today, the businessmen say that it is not possible to do business with complete truth. You eat the food earned by dishonest means and you want that you should get devotion,that there should be peace in the house, and that you should remain healthy. How is this possible? It is not possible to mix oil and water. Similarly, it is not possible to mix truth and untruth. It is required of the mothers also that if wealth and property increases in the house suddenly, they should ask their husbands from where did this wealth come?

"The wife who immerses her husband in luxuries and enjoyment, is not a wife but an enemy. The wife who takes her husband towards truth and religion, she is a true wife."

See, in 'pati-patni' both the letters 'p' and 't' are similar. Even in speaking these, there is a rhythm. In husband-wife, there is not a single letter that is the same. See, as is the culture, so is the language, and so is the life.

Here, the acharya has told us to trust fully on God's capabilities and to do devotion without any desire for fruit. On doing devotion without any desire, a human being is liberated from the bondage of karma. In doing devotion with a desire, the bonds of the karma come in between. We have become clean and have done 'tilak,' now we have become ready to serve God. We did '**sohini seva**' (cleaned the room with a broom). This brooming is not outwardly. This brooming is of our mind. We have to clean our mind.

"O human being, clean the temple of your mind daily."

Clean the temple of your mind where God has to dwell. If the desire for luxuries come into the mind, then the mind will wander and laziness will increase. So, we have to clean our minds with the broom. Then, we have to drink water from the 'jhari ji' and give rise to good thoughts in our mind. In the summers, the jhari ji is covered with a white cloth. In the winters, it is covered with a red cloth. Red clothes symbolise the mother. This jhari ji is mother Yamuna. So, this should be kept on the left side of God. It is not only the jhari, it is the symbol of devotion. Remember, this is not only water, it is devotion incarnate. Remember it is not only water, it is the nectar of devotion. So, when you drink it, say, "O mother Yamuna, if your grace is there, then we will be able to have a glimpse of the ways of God." Only the mother can give the introduction of the father. She is like the mother only –

"**Jai-jai maharani jamuna,**
jai-jai patrani jamuna sundar satwanti naar."

If this incarnation of devotion manifests in your heart, then some symptoms will arise themselves. In this couplet, the worry is that is what I am doing appropriate. My direction is correct or not. See, when you drank the water of the Yamuna, what was the result? You have not served the Lord yet, you have just made the preparations. So, if devotion has arisen in your hearts, you will have an enthusiasm to keep the fast of Ekadashi. The meaning of fast is not only to not eat food grains. The acharya has said–

"**Ekadashi upvaas sarvbhoot daya yatha laabh santoshah sarvendriyo upshamah.**"

This should happen to you also. You should enjoy Ekadashi. There should be no burden in it. There should be enthusiasm in you that today I will keep this fast. God will shower his blessings on me. This feeling should arise. It is said in the Vishnu Puran that in the Kaliyug Kali (discord) resides in food-grains onEkadashi day. So, it is suggested that, one should not eat grains that day. Otherwise, the meaning of fast is to not only remain hungry –

"**Dhan ekadashi, ekadashi kariye to vaikunth paaiye.**"

The sages knew that this human being either works for profit or for greed. So, they have joined fasts with moksha. It is necessary to fast for the body to remain healthy also. To eat less and to eat good food is the best option. By discipline, the desires are quietened. By keeping fast, you become closer to God. Your lust is quietened.

If there are the blessings of Yamuna ji, then there will be enthusiasm in the fast. There are three types of people in this world. One, who are in a higher category than ours, whether it is by wealth, beauty, or brains, or strength. The second are those, who are equal to us. The third are lower than us. So, when devotion arises in the heart, we will feel happy in seeing those who are above us, not jealous. With those who are equal to us, there will not be a competition, but there will be a desire to take him along and walk beside him. With those who are lower than us, there will not be pride, but pity. If this is so, then you should understand that mother Yamuna has been merciful towards you. These are the symptoms of '**sarvbhoot daya**' (mercy for all)

The third quality as the guru says is '**Yatha labh santustho.**" Meaning, you should be satisfied with what you have received. When Bali pleaded with Vaman Dev (priest) to ask for more, then the priest who was an incarnation of God said –

"**Yatha labh santushto.**" Meaning, O Bali, a sanayasin should be happy with what he gets. If you want to be happy, don't think of what you have not got, be happy with what you have got. "**Yadrichaya labh santushtho**." In the end, "**Sarveindriya upshamah.**" Meaning, quieten all your senses. That is why Valmiki maharaj has said-

Jinh ke shravan samudra samana!
Katha tumhari subhag sari nana
Lochan chaatak jinh kari raakhe,

rahhi daras jaldhar abhilashe
Kar nit karhi ram pad pooja,
ram bharose hridaya nahi dooja
Charan ram tirath chali ja hi,
ram bashu tinh ke man mahin
Jinke kapat dabhe nahi maya,
tinke hriday bashu raghu raya.

Sarvendriya upshamah:

If the blessings of Yamuna are with you, then this event will happen. That is why service is done of the jhari ji. Don't think it to be only water. When we pray during the evenings, then at the time of doing 'pranayam' (yogic breathing exercise) while doing '**kumbhak purak rechak**' (religious ritual) we should have this feeling in our mind that at the time of doing 'kumbhak' God is entering inside me. While doing 'kumbhak' his image should be stable in your mind. While doing 'rechak' keep the feeling in your mind that all the impurity of my mind is coming out. 'Jhari ji' alias mother Yamuna is showering her blessings on us. Devotion is coming inside me. While drinking the water of Yamuna, this feeling should be in your mind. Now after doing service of the 'jhari ji', we will do service of the idol of God. It does not matter what the idol of God is made of, whether it is stone or metal, the important thing is the emotion. '**Bhavo hi vidhate deva.**' (God sees the emotion only). So, only the emotion is important.

There are three seasons – summer, rainy, and winter seasons. In the winter season, you should bathe the idol of God completely. It is the order of the guru that when it is extremely cold, the idol of God should be bathed completely only on Saturdays. On the other days, take a clean cloth and wipe the idol and change the clothes. Otherwise, God can catch a cold. In the other two seasons, you should bathe the idol of God daily. The water that should be used for bathing the idol of God depends on the season. How will you test if the water is appropriate for bathing God? Take some water in your hand and touch the elbow of your other hand to it. If it feels alright on touching with the elbow, then it is appropriate. The temperature of the water should neither be too hot nor too cold. Then, after throwing away that water, clean your hands. Next, install the idol of God on a four-cornered stool. There are different traditions among devotees of bathing God; somebody bathes Him with '**panchamrit**' (a mixture containing milk, curd, sugar, honey, and clarified butter), some bathe him with only milk, and some with water. But, one should bathe him keeping in mind one's wealth and power. Don't follow anyone. You should not borrow money from anyone to bathe him. Manu Maharaj has said that 'yagnas' etc. should be done only when you have enough money to look after the needs of your family for the whole year.

"**Bhagwan padarth bhogya nahin bhav bhogya hai.**"

Meaning, God does not look at the materials and paraphernalia, but at the 'emotions' (BHAV) of a devotee.

Don't offer a 56-course meal to God on seeing someone else do it. Your butter and sugar is also enough. You can't decorate Him with flowers everyday, doesn't matter. Just decorate him with your emotions. While bathing the idol, sing with emotion –

Jamuna jal man kesar gholu snan karaoon shyamada,
Kum-kum kera tilak lagaoon pritam dhara bhal ma.
Albeli aankhon man aanju anjan dhara aankh man,
Mor mukut maathe pahiraoon murli rakhoon haath man.
Nazar na laage mahare shyam
sundar nu tapka kar laaoon galma,
Hansati jaoon vaate jaoon naachi uthu taal ma.
Krishna kripalu nirakhi shobha
vaari jaoon mahara balman,
Jamuna jal man kesar...

While bathing the idol of God, you should have the feeling in mind that this is not the idol but God himself. This is the child form of God. A child has soft body parts. So, serve God with gentle hands. While serving God, there is no man, all are gopis. A gopi is "one who hides God in her heart and loves him." As a mother looks after a child, you should serve the idol of God similarly. While looking after a child, tears well up in the eyes of the mother. If while serving God, tears of love do not well up in your eyes, then what sort of service is this? If in the sweets that are offered to God, there are no basil leaves (*Tulsi*), then God does not even look at that offering. Similarly, while serving and worshipping God, if tears are not there, then God does not accept that worship.

"**Nisi din barsat nayan hamare.**

Sada rahat pavas ritu in par jab te shyam sidhare." If the tears of happiness and love do not come into your eyes, then the service is incomplete. Next, wipe the idol with a clean cloth and start decorating the idol. While decorating the idol also, keep in mind your capability. It is not that the beauty of the idol of God increases only with valuable jewellery. The beauty of God is sublime beauty. Surdas has said, "**Hari maine dekho nang dharanga**." Meaning, God is beautiful even without the clothes and the jewellery. God Ram who is sitting on the royal throne is equally beautiful as God Ram who had worn the clothes of a sage while living in 'panchvati' forest. He will shower his blessings on us only if we decorate His idol with expensive clothes, this is not so. He is beauty incarnate Himself, whether you decorate Him or not. He roams in the house of mother Yashoda without any ornaments. We decorate Him only so that some beauty comes into our heart. We raise slogans hailing God so that our faults, our bad habits are quietened. We also decorate God only so that our thinking improves. Our mind is crooked like a hunch-backed woman. On putting the 'tilak' on the idol of God, maybe its crookedness will vanish. How beautiful is he–

"**Varhapidam natwar vapu karanyon karnikaram**
Vibhadra vaas kanakpisham vaijayanti ch malam
Strdhan venu adhar sudhya puryan
Vrindaranyam swapadramanam pravishad geetkirti"

–*Shrimadbhagwat*

Bhajman narayan narayan narayan
satyanarayan narayan narayan
Shriman narayan narayan.
Dwarkadheesh ki jai jai jai jai shri radhe.

✻ CHAPTER 6 ✻

Shrimadvallabhacharya says –

"Loke swasthayam yatha vede haristu na karishyati
Pushti marg stitho yasmatsakshivo bhavtakhilah."

–Sixth couplet

Lord Shri Krishna is the protector of law and order and goodness. He is the incarnation of justice. There should be only one feeling in the mind of a person who has dedicated everything to God– "God, I am Yours, without You I have no life." The soul has been born in the human form, this is the only form in which reason exists. In the other forms of life, one does not have the faculty to reason. Due to this capability to reason, the human beings can adopt a religious way of life and improve their life on this earth, as well as their afterlife.

"Religion is that, on adopting which, a human being benefits."

"Today, there are many holy men in this world, but the religious men are very few."

People know all the rules of the religion, they can explain them very well also. If the explanation remains limited to paper only, then the person cannot reach his goal. A human being should not discard religion under any condition. "Religion means that behaviour which we should adopt constantly." How should our behaviour be in business, in family, in society – this is religion. The great men have called meditation, rituals, and worship as religion. These are only parts of religion, they are not complete religion. If you experience peace in helping a poor man, then you are religious. Our deeds should be such that we don't have to go to the temple. The one who lives in the temple should Himself come to us. This event has happened in life also.

In the Gita, God has said, "O Arjun, what you eat, the 'yagnas' that you do, the charity that you do, dedicate everything to me. Meaning, that all our deeds should be dedicated to God, all our deeds should be done keeping God in mind. When this thought comes into your mind that whatever deed I do should bring happiness to God, then first of all, you will get freedom from sin. If in the shop, you think your customer to be an incarnation of God and behave with him accordingly, then you will never try to cheat your customer.

The wealth that is earned from bad means brings sorrow. It spoils your death. It increases pain and ill-feeling in life. It makes life full of terror. Life should be fearless. Whatever deed you do– eating, bathing, sleeping, or studying – God should be in the centre of everything. In your hands, ears, tongue God should be with you. Always the memory of God should be in your mind. You should never be separate from Him. Whatever deed you do, there is only one feeling behind that – you want to give happiness to your soul. The external deeds are only a drama. Behind everything, is the desire to get permanent happiness. But remember, your happiness lies not in your attempts to find happiness, but in your heart. Its ultimate form is the truth.

According to the scriptures, there is a soul in this body. Before this body, it was somewhere else. After this, it will go somewhere else. These three states are true. The soul is the epitomisation of truth. It remains happy in truth only. If you speak lies, then your soul becomes sad. Happiness does not lie in those resources with which you wish to buy happiness.

"Your running is correct, but your direction is wrong." "Your yearning is correct, but your search is wrong. You want permanent peace in things, which are momentary. This world is the epitomisation of sorrow. It is said in the Shrimadbhagwat:

"**Asar khalu sansar dukh rupi vimohakah.**"

Without adopting religion, permanent peace is impossible. As soon as the mirage of the desires diminishes, even your wife will discard you. What illusion are you under? A person becomes proud with even a little bit of worldly achievements. He becomes drowned in a sea of pride about his beauty, knowledge, power, or family.

"A person's downfall is not as much due to his lust, anger, or greed; as it is due to his pride."

An intelligent person is one who does not let pride engulf him. It is the time of morning. The acharya is sitting peacefully with a happy countenance. He has worn two plain clothes, there is no show or pretence anywhere. By living with simplicity, you will save yourself from sin, because if greed grows, sin grows, and if sin grows, pain grows.

The guru is sitting in a resolute pose. The happiness within is clearly evident on his face. The face is the mirror of the mind. He is a dedicated person. God is everything to him. A human being who has surrendered everything, what worry does he have? When God is capable of everything, then what worry does he have? If you don't have faith in any worship or meditation, then only the action itself is futile. If the emotion is removed from any worship, then the action itself is useless.

Some devotees are sitting in front. They look worried. So, the guru asks them, "Dave ji, **kutshchinta bhavan**?" Meaning, what is the worry, Dave ji? So, Dave ji said, "Maharaj, what should I do? Whatever business I undertake, I suffer losses in that. Nobody in my family respects me. Wherever I go, I get disrespect only. There is no respect for me in the society also. If I ask anyone for help, I do not get it. Maharaj, why is my fate so twisted?" A good guru is merciful, is generous. If the guru does not understand the problem of the disciple, then who will understand? A good guru walks along with us.

It is the right of the disciple to go to the guru. But, you should remember that there should be no needless intrusions in the daily routine of the great men. The time of great men is very precious.

So, it should not be wasted needlessly. Those who do not understand the value of time, time destroys such persons. Don't always talk about your sorrows with God or your guru, talk about your happiness also sometimes. Guruji, now I find that I enjoy doing my worship. Tell him this also. Don't ask for any worldly thing from the great men. If someone fulfils your worldly desires, then he is not a good guru, he is a magician.

So, in response to Dave ji's question, the noble guru, Vallabhacharya said –

"Loke swasthayam ......bhavitakhilah."

O Dave ji, if the soul has really surrendered completely before God, then understand that God will put obstacles in his worldly and Vedic path. Why is this so? If some obstacles come in your business, or some problems come in your health, or you do not get the fruits of your hard work, then understand that God is going to give you some other happiness, which is out of this world. If unhappiness comes in the life of evil men, then this is not the blessing of God, but this is the fruit of their deeds. But, if you have dedicated yourself completely to God, and then also you are not getting prestige in the society, then understand that God is soon going to have mercy on you. This event has happened in Mirabai's life. The world will speak, will oppose you, will criticise you, then understand that this is according to God' will. God wants to lift you up from ego and attachment. He wants to free you of these evils. Till you are not free of these evils, you cannot be close to God. God wants to free you of them, so this event will happen. Only then will you be able to achieve God.

Maane sachidanand var payo he ji man
Gagan mandal mahara sasra ji...

All the people in this world are experiencing the fruit of their deeds. Pain and failure are due to the result of your deeds also. But, if you have dedicated everything and still get pain and failure, then understand that God is embracing you.

The principle of 'karma' is very true. After making it once, even God does not interfere in it. If you did some deed due to your selfishness, if you did it to satisfy your senses and you got failure as a result of that, then understand that it was a fruit of your deeds. If any obstacle comes in the path of dedicated souls like Saint Tukaram, then understand that God is doing this so that he does not become too greatly immersed in his worldly role. God is doing this so that he does not stop due to the attachment towards his son or wife. That is why this incident has happened. So, what is happening in the life of Tukaram is the blessings of God. And what is happening in the life of Fokat Lal is the fruit of his deeds. Because what Tukaram is doing, he is doing keeping God in mind. God will become happy with this deed of mine, this feeling is in his mind. Worship is my 'karma', my religion. This is the feeling in his mind. And what Fokat Lal is doing, he is doing for his family. My friend spent two crores for his daughter's wedding, so I will spend three crores.

Here, we are talking about dedicated people, those who have formed a relationship with God. The feeling in their mind is 'Naath tavaasmi' 'Nath dasoaham' (God, I am yours; God I am your servant.) According to the worldly traditions, people worship the God and Goddess who is the deity of their family. This is a worldly tradition. Or, they worship God according to the Vedic traditions, like doing the traditional worship, going for a trip to holy places, 'yagnas' etc. But, if God does not let even this be successful, then what should the devotee do? Vallabhacharya has said a very beautiful thing for this. There are four types of labours that we have to perform – (1) Dharma (religion), (2) Arth (wealth), (3) Kaam (desire), (4) Moksha (liberation). But, the definition of labour has changed for the devotees – My 'religion', is to serve God. My 'wealth', is the name of God. My 'desire', is to see God. My 'moksha' – is to attain God. In their lives, service is this only. The main aspect of service is not deed, but surrender. Without surrender, there is no service. In service, the resources are meaningless, love is the main thing. So, the acharya is saying that in the 'pushti' way of worship, the feeling of servility is there. But, the meaning of servility is not being a servant only, but the feeling is "God, you are my everything. My happiness lies in your happiness." Like there is a two-month old child, the mother looks after it after moment. The child does not do anything in return, does not give anything. But, still the mother serves him. Because she gets happiness out of that service. Similarly, you should also serve God in this way.

One gentleman asked, "God is the lord of the whole world, then how can he become a child?" Yes, he can become. God can become a child also. God is capable of doing anything. Although the God of Vedanta does not belong to anyone, he is just an ever pure element, which has no form, no smell, and no shape. He does not love anyone, nor does he hate anyone, nor does he inspire anyone. Like, when we light the earthen lamp at night, then in the light of the lamp, some people may eat food, some may read books, some may decorate themselves, some may steal. The duty of the lamp is to only give the light. It does not give you any inspiration that you read a book or steal. Similarly, according to the Vedanta, God is unattached. After giving birth to you, he has become detached. Whatever deeds you do, he is a mute spectator. He does not inspire you that you do this or that –

"**Nag pekhan tum pekhani hare vidhi hari**
shambhu nachavan hare."

Meaning, the world is a stage. God is the spectator. He does not interfere in the drama. As a spectator simply watches the drama, similarly God also watches only. But, if the devotees makes that formless, qualityless entity their son, brother, husband, or father, he is ready to become all these. It is said in the Gita

Ye yatha mam prapadyante taansthtaiva bhajamyaham...

Meaning, as one worships me, I take that form. As the emotion in your mind is, I take that form. So, what was the emotion in Vallabhacharya's mind – it was the Lord carrying the Goverdhan mountain in his hands. So, God, Srinath ji's form is of stone. God emerged from stone because the devotee's mind was there. So, the name of the Lord who carried the Goverdhan mountain in his hands is Srinath ji. With love, we call him Shri ji. But, otherwise,

God says I don't have any form. Whatever form the devotee gives me, I take that form. As water has no form, shape, or smell; but if you keep water in any utensil, it takes the form of that utensil. So, if you see him in the form of your son, or your father then he takes that form. In Gita, Arjun asked Krishna, "Who are you?" He said, "I am death, who has come to finish everyone here. Here, no one is mine. Whether you fight or not, everyone here is going to be finished. You are just a medium." So, God has no form. "**Bhaktabhilasha charitanusari.**" Otherwise, God accepts the form of a child because whether the child is our own or someone else's, he is a subject of everyone's love. He is guileless, sinless, he attracts a person immediately. Service is my religion, and my wealth is the name of God. The guru says that the wealth of the devotees is God's name. Their work is the desire to see God. As the '**chatak**' bird does not drink the water of the ocean. It only drinks the water of the '**swati nakshatra**' (name of a constellation), similarly it is the desire of the devotee that God should live in my heart-

Lochan chaatak jimi kari raakhe.....

Such a devotee sees God in every human being. When his separation pangs at being separated from God become too great, the guru asks not only people, but also stones, and the river, "Have you seen 'Radha Vallabh' (an epithet of Krishna)?" Without suffering the pangs of separation, the devotion is not complete. Sitting alone, a person should cry daily and pray, "God, if only I could see you once."

"Jayati tedhikam janmana vraja shrayat indira shashavadtrahi."

(Gopi–Geet)

Meaning, your desire should only be to see God. There should be no other desire in the mind of the seeker. "See the world not with the eyes of lust, but with the eyes of Ram." This world is beautiful. If you have this feeling in your mind, then sin will come in. God is beautiful. If you have this feeling in your mind, then goodness will start. The only difference is in the way of seeing things.

Vallabhacharya is saying that I don't want to become God. Like the Vedantists say, "Aham Brahmaasmi" (I am God), we don't want this. We want our own separate identity. God and we should be face-to-face with each other. We should be able to see each other. As the gopis say, "God, you just appear in front of us. We only want to see you playing, playing the flute, and grazing the cows. If we are able to achieve moksha, then what will we get? If we are able to achieve moksha, then we can't see or speak, or see. After we go to heaven, we are not going to get this happiness. So, God, we don't want to go to heaven.

Lokey swasthayam tatha vedey haristu na karishayati,
Pushti margam stitho yasmatsakshinon bhavitaakhila.

Meaning, God will separate you from the worldly and the Vedic traditions. This does not mean that we should leave the worldly and the Vedic traditions. Vedic path is the path of goodness. If we leave this path, it will be a sacrilege. The guru says, "No, I am not taking you towards inaction. I am taking you towards God." Because what is religion? Once in the book 'Narayan Upanishad', Narad ji went to God. Narad ji cleaned the feet of God. God withdrew his feet. Narad ji said, "God, what is this? I am your devotee. I wanted to wash your feet. Why did you do this?" So, what reply did God give?

"**Aham dharamasya vaktaham kartadnumodita**
Tacchiksayam lokmim matidaputrmaanravid."

Meaning, O son, "**maan ravid**", don't be sad. You don't understand religion. I am the speaker. I am the doer. I am the protector of religion. I am the supporter of religion. So, Krishna is the religion. Our senses and deeds all are Krishna (**Krishna ev gatimarmam –3**). This incident is given here, so that nobody misunderstands the guru.

Devotion is that which grows everyday.

Sitaram charan rati morey anudit baith anugrah torey.

As still water starts smelling, similarly devotion should also not become still. Devotion should be renewed everyday. Like love is renewed everyday. If compromise comes into service and worship, you should understand that your devotion has become stale. If the time of offering sweets to God is five minutes past 10, then you should do this at this time only. God said to Narad ji, "Don't be sad. After coming to God, there should be no desires left, as after coming near the Kalpvriksh the desires are fulfilled themselves." So, Vallabhacharya ji says –

Moksh krishnasth chetdhruvam – Meaning, our moksha is the attainment of God. God is everything. He is religion. He is everything.

Jai jai murari girivardhari kunj vihari sukhkari
Kar basi dhaari go van chari tav gatinyari tapdhari
Radhe shyam shyam shyam, radhe shyam shyam shyam.
Avichal avinashi vishv vilasi ghat-ghat vaasi pusprashi
Arimaadik daasi alakhat kaashi purn prakashi jag vaasi
Jai jai murari.....
Radhe shyam....

He will free you from the worldly traditions and the Vedic rites and from devotion done with the desire for fruit, and will make you do devotion done without any desire. Because, if devotion is done with the desire for a fruit, and the devotee does not get that fruit, then he is drowned in a sea of sorrow. The acharya wants to free the godly man from sorrow. Most people want to do work with a desire for the fruits of that work and want to obtain happiness by this means. But, on being unsuccessful, they cry. Keep this treasure of tears for God. You have cried for your husband and your son, you have cried for this world, you have cried for prestige, you have cried for money. Cry once for God and see. Here, the meaning of freeing from worldly traditions and Vedic rites is to free one from devotion done with a motive. Devotion done with a motive is a reason for sorrow. In the Gita, God has said –

Dhyayato vishyanpuns sangasteyshupujaayate
Sadat sajayate kamah kamatkrodhobhijayate
Krodhat bhavati sammoh sammoaha tasmriti vimrayah
Smritibhrshot buddhi nasho buddhi nashat pranshayasati.

–Gita para 2, couplet 62

So, God wants to take you out of this vicious circle. So, God creates obstacles in the path of the godly man. He wants human beings to fall in love with the soul instead of the material things. The material things have their limits, the soul is limitless. So, when you get failure in the worldly tasks, how should the human being understand that I am moving towards God. For this, God has said in the Gita –

Vidya Vinay sampanne brahmane gavi hastini
Shuni chaiv shwapakey ch panditah sam darshinih.

–Gita para 5, couplet 18

Dukheshunudwigana manah sukheshu vigat spriah
Veetrag bhaya krodhah stith dhi mruniruchayate.

–Gita para 2, couplet 56

So, if the soul has dedicated itself to God, so whether sorrow comes or happiness, if his mind remains stable, then he will become a wise person. If you are able to tell the height of the Himalayas, the depth of the ocean, and why a person falls sick; then this is not knowledge, this is bookish knowledge, this is cleverness. "**Knowledge is that which destroys even the smallest of bad thought.**" What is the goal of human beings? Good food, good dress, sleep. Is this the goal of life? There is something more to life also – **Dharmohi tesham adhikovishcsho dharmehina pashu samana.** Meaning, without religion, human beings are like animals. Even animals do all these.

Understand the value of human life. "**You have spent your life in getting ready for life.**" Like a person was roaming around with a cot on his head. Someone asked him, "What will you do with this?" He said, "If I get the time, I will put it down and sleep on it." So, is life only to carry around a burden like this? If we don't have wealth, even then we can laugh.

So, on obtaining knowledge, a person will become dispassionate and free from worldly attachments. On obtaining knowledge, we don't try to accumulate unnecessarily. On accumulating unnecessarily, the worry to keep it safely will increase. As much as you will accumulate, your peace will leave you. A knowledgeable person becomes free from all fears. "**If there is no attachment, there is no fear. If there is no desire, there is no anger.**" Such a person is called a sage. So, if adversity comes into your life, tell God, not the worldly men. Although, he knows everything. Yes, if you go and sit near Him, then he will know that you have faith in Him. Then, he will fulfil all your desires. He said to Sugreev –

"**Sakha soch tyaghu bal morey, sab vidhi kaaj ghatab main torey.**" Meaning, I will do all your work, so why are you worrying?

Abhi bhareli nazaro hai rakhyo mewar na shrinath ji
Charan kamal maan shish navavi darsan karoon shrinath ji
Daya kariney bhalti dejo mewar na shrinath ji
Hoon dukhiyare thaare dwaare aavi no shrinath ji
Thaare bharose jivan naiya haath dharo na shrinath ji
Ant samay ni arji hamari sanmukh rahyo shrinath ji
Vaikunth aapo charane rakho mewar na shrinath ne

So, sit in front of God and open your heart. The soul becomes free on doing this. Seek the company of those people who have achieved this type of knowledge. There can never be a mistake in God's justice. Human beings make mistakes. If the body is strong, it immerses itself in luxuries. Gods blessings come in the form of sweets also and in the form of medicines also. Yes, even in the form of bitter medicine does God shower his blessings. God does not know how to strike down, he only knows how to save. He will not drown you. If adversity comes, don't become a beggar who begs from door to door. Meaning, don't ever get priests and astrologers to propitiate the planets. You will not get happiness from that. Offer God strengthening foods like milk and fruits, and such foods which bring happiness. Offer God such foods which are juicy, soft, and tasty. What does Krishna like –

"**Bala ne makhan bhave re, bala ne misri bhave re....**
Jai jai shri radhe – 3"

* CHAPTER 7 *

"Sevakriti guro agya badhan va harichaya,
Atah sevaparam chitam vidhaya sthiyatam sukham."

–Seventh couplet

"Chitodweg vidhayapi hariaryachat karishyati
Tathaiv tasya lileti matva chintam drutam tyajet."

–Eighth couplet

Lord Shri Krishna is extremely merciful. He fulfils all the desires of the devotees. Those godly men who have dedicated themselves to God, God tells the thoughts of His heart only to them. The means to know the thoughts of God's heart is service. By doing service, the mind becomes pure, the human being becomes free of his sins. By doing service, the mind is purified, the world appears as a house of God. Those who serve the Lord, not only become peaceful themselves, but those who come close to that person, they also attain peace of mind. If there is no surrender in the service, then the service is not fruitful. If there is ego in the mind of the person doing the service, then he will not enjoy doing the service. He will not get the blessings of God. The person who serves God should think that even the wicked person is a part of God, so I should keep a feeling of mercy and friendship towards him also. A godly man has to remain cautious 24 hours of the day. Worldly desires are very strong. Even the devotee can come under their spell. The biggest obstacle to service is luxuries. Whether it is the luxuries of the body, or of fulfilling the senses, or happiness of family members, or prestige in the society; this is the biggest obstacle to service. The emotion behind service is to provide happiness to God. A godly man should follow the rules very cautiously and patiently. The world is full of good and bad qualities. The human soul has to live in the world, so he cannot escape its goodness or badness. The only way to escape these is to take shelter with God. Surrender your material body and your soul to God. While doing service, your mind should not be upset or worried, only then will the service be fruitful.

The guru knows the condition of the human being. He knows that the mortal and resourceless human being spends all his life in pain and illness.

"**As soon as pain and illness come in, happiness and peace go away.**" Pain is due to attachment. Illness is not only of the body, but also of the mind. Raman Maharishi got gangrene. Everyone told him to ask God to remove it. Maharishi said, "Doesn't God know of this?" People asked him, "Then, what is the reason for this?" He replied, "Due to this, my relationship with God will continue." This is the fruit of sorrow. In happiness, a human being forgets God. Maybe, if she had been in Ayodhya, Sita would not have remembered God as much as she did while sitting in 'ashok vatika' (garden). Hanuman ji described in what condition was Sita sitting there-

"**Krish tanu sees jata ek beni japat hriday raghupati gun shreni.**" So, if you get too immersed in your worldly tasks, or get too much happiness, then your attention can be diverted from God. So, if happiness is taking a human being who has dedicated himself to God, away from God; then God will take you far away from that happiness. Our religion is to hand over the body, mind, heart everything to God. To do devotion while living in the family is a test of true devotion. The test of the tree's strength is during storms, not during the summer season. The test of a human being is that he should remember God during happiness also.

Now, in devotion, we have done the service of the 'jhari' also. Now, comes the time to offer sweets to God. "**Jatha dehe,**

tatha gehe." Meaning, as the human body wants, so does God. You should take the permission of your guru and serve God as your guru tells you to. Don't do according to your will. The order of the guru is your licence to serve God. Due to this, you don't have the fear of making a mistake. Otherwise, it has been said in the Gita what type of meals should be offered to God-

"**Aayuh satv balarogya sukham preeti vardhanah**
Rasyah snigdhah sthira hridha aaharah satvik priyah."

–Gita 17th chapter

God likes simple and pure food only. Strong food is that in which there is no nutrition. A meal that has been prepared more than four hours ago is stale and un-nutritious. More spicy, salty, or dry food is also not good food. Bad food is one on eating which the mind becomes fickle.

So, give God dry fruits, which increase the life span. The mind is like a sick person. If ever a person starts feeling proud of his wealth or luxuries, so you should understand that his mind has become sick. There is only way to escape this and that is "**Krishna eva gatirmam.**"

In this machine age, all paths have been destroyed and have become filled with wickedness. The world is a mine of disease. There is neither purity of the system, nor there is power in the mantras, neither have the holy places remained holy, neither have the holy men remained holy. In such a situation, the only way for the human beings to survive is to surrender before God. Don't use wealth, become the sons of wealth, then wealth will not trouble you, but will nurture you. Wealth is not faithful to anyone except God. God himself says, "**Mam maya durtyaya.**" God has given you wealth only so that you serve God with it.

"**God has given you this wealth not for enjoyment, but for devotion.**" On enjoying the luxuries of life, not only the body, but the mind also becomes diseased. Many births have to be spent to again make it come alive.

"**There is momentary happiness in enjoyment, but there is permanent happiness in sacrifice.**"

Sit before God and tell him all your troubles. Become a child in front of God, never become the seeker. Only god is capable, human beings are always incomplete. Remember, in this path of devotion, never trust your mind and intelligence. The one who relies on his brains, God never gives his blessings to those. Surrender all your sorrows and happiness to God. My tongue should always chant your name. My eyes should always see you. My ears should hear the glory of your character always. My hands should serve you. My feet should always go towards holy places. Then, God will heal you. Don't ever try for yourself or for luxuries. Otherwise your mind will become stricken with lust. If your desires are not fulfilled, you will feel angry. Your memory will be destroyed and in the end, your life will be destroyed.

If you become a man of God, then unhappiness will never come into your life – it doesn't happen like this. Adversities come in the life of men of God also. But, if a human being has dedicated himself to God, then he becomes detached. His mind becomes stable. If our guru is a dear person of God's, then we can also become dear to God. "**Don't sing the praises of holy men, instead try to imbibe their good qualities.**" If you follow the teachings of the saints and the sages, then your life will become successful. Don't follow worldly people. God has said in the Gita, "Everything is attainable to me, but still I take the form of human beings, do deeds for the welfare of human beings, so that other people get the inspiration." You should pray to God that even if good things do not happen by these hands, then atleast anything bad should not be done by these hands. There is no prayer, which is not heard. You should have faith –

"**Kabhunk deen dyal bhanak padegi kaan.**" Meaning, someday God will listen to your prayers.

So, today the devotee is worried. Dave ji is keeping his worry in front of the guru, "Gurudev, we always follow your orders. But, if we surrender everything to God, will God also order us some day? If someday, God orders us, should we listen to God or should we listen to you?"

The meaning of 'Upanishad' is to 'sit close', to sit close to God. Sit close to the guru and ask him questions, in a gentle manner "**Pranipaten pariprashnen**....." If he is a good guru, he will definitely answer you. To remove the doubts of the disciple is the duty of the guru. A good guru will remove your illusions, he will tell you a path. It is not his work to walk on that path for you. A good guru does not show you miracles. He doesn't do your worldly tasks. So, don't take your worldly problems to the great men.

The great man, Vallabhacharya, is merciful. On the question of the disciple that will God order me, he replied, "Yes, he will definitely do it." So, the devotees asked, "Then, what should we do? Should we obey the order of the guru or God?" If sometimes, God himself appears and orders you, then also its not disregarding the orders of the guru. Like in 'Bhakt Maal', the guru told a devotee to do a mental service "to fan the Lord with a hand fan". So, the disciple used to close his eyes daily and used to mentally fan the Lord daily. One day, when a meal was being offered to God, the devotee was fanning him mentally. Suddenly, God appeared himself and said to the devotee, "Son, open your eyes. I am standing in front of you." The devotee, "No, if I open my eyes, then my mental fanning service will stop. And the comfort that you are getting due to my fanning you, that will stop. So, I will not open my eyes."

The biggest speciality of this 'Kaliyug' is that if you remember God with a true heart for even half a moment, then it is not difficult to attain God. All the devotees sang-

Keshava madhava he deva madhusudana....

Remember God at all times. Remember, "**Tasmat sarveshu kaleshu mamanusmar**". Yes, if in the beginning, due to some worldly tasks, the seeker forgets God for some time, then he can express regret in his heart and ask forgiveness from God. God is merciful, he will forgive you. Immerse your mind in God again. Don't become stricken by an inferiority complex that I forgot God. Tell God, "God, I am a resourceless, mortal human being. Have mercy on me. Only then will I be able to remember you."

If God has mercy on us, then we can live a family also and worship God. In today's time, there is no place which is free from sin, where will you go? It is better that wherever you are, however you are, as long as you live, remember God.

"**Jis dham mein jis kaam mein jis haal mein raho**
Radha raman Radha raman Radha raman kaho.
Maan mein apmaan mein samman mein raho
Radha raman Radha raman Radha raman kaho."

If your family members oppose, then do mental devotion. Don't worship God in front of them. Along with this, pray to God to give good sense to your family members, so that they do not remain against you, so that they do not put obstacles in your worship. '**Grihasthashram**' (one of the phases of life according to the Vedas in which a person should live the life of householder) is that only till God is being worshipped in it. If the husband and wife do not worship God, then it is not a good household, it is only an arrangement. If both the husband and wife pray together, then only is it a successful household. In our religion, a wife is a 'dharam patni' (wife according to the religion), she is not wife only. This means that she supports us in our religious works. Now, someone may say that if both of them immerse themselves in worship, then who will fulfil the worldly duties? The great guru has made arrangements for that also. The great guru says that among the four parts of the day, serve God only during one part. The rest of the three parts, do your worldly duties. Like Vidur ji used to do. Vidur ji never used to sit in the court of the Kauravas. He used to go there only when called. He used to complete his work there and come back. He used to sit with his wife, Sulabha, and serve God. He did not have any children. People used to call mother Sulabha mad. All the time, she used to remain immersed in her love for God. She used to put perfume on her hands and serve God. "God, so that my hands become soft, lest you should be hurt by my rough hands."

Why is it necessary to take the permission of the guru before serving God? The great guru says –

"**Sevakritiguroragya badhanam va harichaya.**"

On taking the guru's permission before service, you are saved from all blame. There are many faults due to which the progress lessens. According to Vedanta, the meaning of progress is "to not be swept away in the flow." Otherwise, usually, people do some things just on seeing other people do those. If he has kept a fast, so I will also keep. If he has read this scripture, I will also read. This is 'influenced devotion'. This is not natural devotion. Devotion should be natural. Influenced devotion does not grow. Devotion should grow everyday. We don't have to be swept away in the flow of the river. Your devotion, your love towards God is personal. There should be no third person between you and God. If you become so close to God, then he will accept your flowers, fruits everything because God accepts the meal offered with love. So, on taking the permission of a good guru, by being close to a good guru, you become free from all faults and become fit to serve God. "A good guru is one on going close to whom you start remembering God, and your faults go away. Non-violence and love should awaken in you. A good guru is like a physician who treats your faults, like a doctor treats illnesses. It is said in Ramayan–

"**Sadguru vaid vachan vishwasa........**"

Meaning, a good guru is a physician. He gives the medicine to remove faults. He frees you from lust. He will give you a medicine in the form of a mantra. He will tell you the path of devotion. If you will do that, then God will give His blessings to you. If you do it after reading books, you will not get success so easily because in books you will get only the meaning, whereas with a guru you will get the feeling also. So, the great guru says – "**Sevakriti guroragya......**"

If sometimes while serving, you disobey an order of the guru, then tell him. If God gives you an order Himself, then tell the guru. Don't get upset. If he is a good guru, then he will say that it is a good thing. Tell the guru that God has ordered me to do this. The good guru and God both want the welfare of the being. Arjun asks –

"**Kaaparnya doshohat swabhavah prichami**
twam dharm sammud chetah

Yacheya syatrishchitam bruhitanmey
shishyateaham shadhimam twam prapannam."

Meaning, God, I am your disciple. Tell me that path which is beneficial for me. Because, the great guru says –

"**Ekam shastra devki putra geetam**
eko devo devki putr ev
Eko mantrastasya namani yani karmaapyekam
tasya devasya seva."

As we continue to read the Gita, we become more and more mesmerised. So, the acharya has said –

"**Parmanand sambandhey dukham tishtathi naiv.**"

Meaning, if you form a relation with God, then the troubles will not stay.

Our relationships are scattered. It is distributed between society, family, money, and prestige. With some, we have the relationship of love. With some, we have the relationship of hatred. Yes, even if it is a relationship of hatred, it is a relationship. If you form a relationship with God, then there is only benefit in that. Make him your son, husband, father, friend, or enemy anything. There is only your benefit in this. There was a Swami Ramdas in Ayodhya. He used to consider God as his disciple. So, he never used to go to 'Kanak Bhavan'. 'Kanak Bhavan' means the personal residence of Shri Ram. The elders should not go in the personal residence of the younger people. But, worldly people don't understand the great men. They started saying, "Does this happen anywhere? Are you Guru Vashishth?" They took him to 'Kanak Bhavan' forcibly. Ramdas closed his eyes. People said, "Swamiji, see God is standing in front of you." As soon as Swami Ramdas opened his eyes, people saw that the crowns of the idols of Ram, Sita, and Lakshman flew and fell on the feet of Swami Ramdas. God saluted the guru, and Swami Ramdas discarded his body at that very instant.

"**Aiso Ram hai dukh haran aiso Ram hai dukh haran....**
To parmanand sambandhey dukham tishtathi naivam
Krishna seva sadakarye....."

Meaning, if you form a relationship with God, then all your troubles will go away.

The seventh couplet of 'Navrattan Bodh' is like 'indranil' (sapphire). On chanting it daily, your life will be filled with happiness. Greenery will come into your life –

"**Chintadweg vidyayati hariiryadyat karishyati**
Tathaiv tasya leeleti matva chintam drutam tyajyet."

–8th couplet, Navratan Bodh

The devotees are asking the great guru that if we have surrendered everything in our lives, then also sorrow comes into our life, then what should we do? When we have surrendered everything before the Lord, then why does worry, failure, turmoil, and humiliation come into our life still? Then, the great guru said that on surrendering everything, it does not mean that your life will become as you want it to. When you have handed over the reigns of your life to the charioteer, then it is his wish where he takes you. Yes, but you can become free from worry that whatever he does will be for your welfare. Consider that a will of God and discard worry.

"**Tathaiv tasya leeleti matva chintam drut tyajyet.**"

"**When sorrow comes into your life, understand that your sins are lessening; and when happiness comes into your life, understand that the credit that you had accumulated for good deeds is lessening."** See, how the washerman beats the clothes on the stone to clean the clothes. Similarly, God also throws us on the stone of sorrow to cleanse our life. But, remember, he always keeps a hand of his blessings on you also. He will not break you. Have patience. "**Dhairya kanthaa udasin kaupin.**" Meaning, God will listen to you. If the worry continues in the mind of the devotee, his appearance will become like a demon. Due to your impatience, your power, desire, and thinking capabilities will be destroyed. Due to the desire for the fruit, a dullness will come in your service. Due to the worry, a dullness will come in your devotion, disregard may also come in. At such a time, a devotee has to be cautious. Consider everything a game by God and discard all your worries. If in the sorrows of the world also you keep thinking of God, then the poison will become nectar.

Lankini has said in the *'Sundar Kaand'* (a chapter of Ramayana)

"**Pravishi nagar kijai sab kaja hriday raakhi kausalpur raja**
Garal sindhu ripu karhi bhitai, gopad sindhu anal sitlai."

Meaning, if you remember God in your heart, then even the poison will become nectar. As the fruits of poison also became sweet for Hanuman, the fire became cool, and the ocean became like heaven similarly this ocean of suffering and ignorance (bhavsagar) becomes like a heaven. For the person who keeps the image of God in mind while doing a work –

"**Chitram vidhaye sthiyataam sukham.**"

You make your mind stable. If sorrow has come without your asking for it, happiness will also come without your asking for it. This is a predestined circle, it is a natural phenomenon. So, what do we have to do –

"**Saroj netraye kripayutaya mandarmala paribhushitaya**
Udar hasaya lasanmukhaya namostu gopijan vallabhaya."

Meaning, we have to keep thinking of God all the time.

"Ayam sansar dukhasaya nivriti brahm bodhanam."

So, when the devotees asked the question to the teacher, then when our everything belongs to God, then why does turmoil, adversity, and failure come into our life. So, the reason for this is till a person is not able to realise God fully, till then he is not able to be free from sorrow.

See, there are so many holy men in the world today. But, what is the reason that their discourses don't have an effect on the mind of human beings. Such holy men whose voice is able to touch the hearts of the people, such holy men are very few. The reason is that their knowledge is bookish, it is not wisdom. There is no emotion in their voice. That knowledge which is not natural, that discourse which is contrived does not influence us. This is the difference between the voice of the priests and saint Kabir.

When the priests asked Kabir, "Kabir, you are not even literate, but still the people listen to you. Whereas, we have studied the Vedas, but still the people do not listen to us." Kabir said, "**Tu kahta kagaz ki lekhi, main kehta aankhan ki dekhi.**"

Meaning, the knowledge that arises from the heart, not the brain, that is wisdom. "**The knowledge of books is useful in life, but wisdom is useful in life and at the time of death also.**"

"**Sorrow is the mother of wisdom.**" So, the great guru says that sorrow is relieved on getting realisation, or after getting sorrow one achieves realisation. So, when sorrow comes, you don't worry. He is ready to do your welfare.

If lust, anger, greed, and attachment cannot be conquered by discipline, yoga, asanas (yogic exercises), meditation, and pranayam (yogic breathing exercises), then the easiest solution is '**Mukund sevaya**' (meaning serve God). Serve God. Although, there are many people who can do yoga and everyone can offer God meals, bathe him, worship him, chant the mantras, but not all can serve God. Dance like Meera, filled with bliss, in front of him. This is easy. Remember, we are not comparing any two methods over here. The method of yoga has its own place. The method of devotion has its own place. Here, the good guru is telling his experience that though the method of yoga is good, but in today's age it is difficult to follow that method. Then, what should we do? That is why it is said that serving God is the easiest and most excellent method to remove your faults, and there is no other method which is equal to it. Today, how many people can discard this body through meditation (**sahaj samadhi**)? Till you like prestige, post, and priesthood, till then you are sick. And it is a sin to take undue advantage of someone's faith. At the end time, the condition of such people is not good.

"**Tathaiv tasya leeleti matva chintam drutam tyajyet.**"

Consider it a game of his done for your welfare and discard your worry. Just serve him. "**Krishna seva sada karye.**" Meaning, the human being has to serve Him always. If you are too busy in your worldly tasks, then do mental service. God has Himself said that in this world one never gets freedom from worldly duties. Sleeping, sitting, eating all these are also actions. So, when you have to do an action, why not do a good action? Some people are not able to do good deeds. This does not mean that they do not want to do. The reason is that their sins have not been destroyed yet and these stop them from doing good deeds. "**Till your sins are not destroyed completely, till then you cannot walk on the path of devotion.**"

So, what type of meals does God like? Pure, simple, ones which increase intelligence. Fresh, juicy, sweet, ones which gives strength. There is no purity in the things one buys from a market, so those should not be offered to God. Although you may offer a one-course meal instead of a 56-course meal, but the meal should be cooked yourself and should be pure.

After offering the meal, we do the 'aarti' The method of doing the 'aarti' has been told in the Padma Puran (a religious book). The aarti is done of 12 body parts. The 'aarti' is moved in circles in front of five body parts – mouth, chest, hips, knees, and feet. The 'aarti' should be moved in front of these parts only. In some forms of worship, 'aarti' is not done, only devotional songs are sung (kirtan). Devotional songs should always be sung. Even if you cannot sing with the right tune or at the right speed, but you should do 'kirtan' always. God loves 'kirtan' a lot.

Goverdhan giridhar govinda , gokul palak parmananda
Shri vatsankit shri kaustum ghar gaavat bhaya
har paahi mukunda
Anandadik vaaridhi khel adbhut parakram anupam sheel
Shri nandatmaj shritjan palak shri kar
kislaya anand lochan
Goverdhan girdhar govind........

There should be mainly three idols in your temple – one of God, one of the great guru, and the third of Yamuna Maharani. In the 'pushti' form of worship, it is allowed to keep an image of a good guru also in the temple. The guru with whose help you have formed a relation with God, his image is also a form of God. First, you should do 'aarti' of God, then the guru, then Yamuna Maharani. The meaning of 'aarti' is a plea, and also the feeling of giving happiness to God is behind doing it. God, you should not feel too warm, neither should you feel too cold, we have to take care of this also. You should not light an 'akhand deepak' (an earthen lamp which keeps burning continuously, which is never extinguished) in front of God. God is light himself, then what need does he have for light. And then, if God touches the earthen lamp, then what? So, the lamp should be kept away from God. Even while doing 'aarti' keep the earthen lamp away. The 'aarti' should be done with emotion.

Aarti srinath ji vandana karron prabhu ni kripa karoon
Ghanan ghanan ghanta baje prabhu aarti saji
prabhu aarti saji
Dhal na mridang aadi bansuri saji prabhu bansuri saji
Aarti shrinath vandan karoon prabhu vandana karoon....
Dwarikadheesh ki jai, balkrishna lal ki jai
Om namo parvati pataye har har mahadev.
Jai jai shri radhe –3
Shri vrindavan vihari lal ki jai.

✻ CHAPTER 8 ✻

Shrimad Vallabhacharya says –

Tasmat sarvattam na nityam shri krishnah sharnam mam
Vaddwirevam sattam stheyamityev me matih.

–Ninth couplet

Lord Shri Krishna is eternal bliss. He is a well-wisher of the beings. It is difficult to attain God without walking on the path of devotion. Without entering into the path of devotion (bhakti marg), it is not possible to become close to God. You can enter the path of devotion only with the blessings of a good guru. No being can enter into the path of devotion (bhakti marg) independently. After entering into the devotional path, the interest towards God is possible only by the blessings of God. The throne of devotion is humility. There should not be a feeling in the devotee that I am the best, the rest of the people are sinners, and unintelligent, I am knowledgeable, I am a seeker. This is an obstacle in the path of devotion, because in the path of devotion no one is superior. In Navdha Bhakti, there are some types of devotion, which a person cannot do in this machine age. So, if faith is not there, then the seeker can deviate from this path. The good qualities that are needed of a devotee are humility, wisdom, simplicity, and no feeling of false pride. The sign of a devotee is that he salutes everyone. If the blessings of God are not there, then fate, death, 'karma' will all create trouble. When the ego arises, the human being starts considering himself superior on this path of devotion.

After entering into the path of devotion, when you have dedicated yourself to God, you have surrendered everything to God, then where is the place of ego. By serving God, you get good sense. Due to the blessings of God, a human being becomes able to serve God. In the present times, good sense and wealth cannot co-exist together. Too much wealth brings diseases and pain. If one has too much wealth, he falls in love with the luxuries. One does not fall in love with the Lord then. If God wants to shower his blessings on you, he does not give wealth, but he gives good sense. Human beings have always lost in front of wealth. So, that wealth is not able to touch the soul, God separates the human being from his wealth. When God separates the human being from his wealth, the human being thinks that sorrow has come upon him. It is not so. God is going to shower his special blessings on you, so he has made this arrangement. Ask God to give you sorrows like mother Kunti. With too much happiness, life is wasted. A person starts cheating another person, thinks himself to be the best. In sorrow, a person loses his pride. He remembers God. "**The path of wealth is dear, but the path of good sense is the better path.**"

God gives good sense when a human being strives to attain God. The meaning of striving to attain God is "**To establish God in the mind.**" By establishing God in the mind, the thoughts become pure. His devotion bears fruit and the human being is in a state of bliss throughout the day. God said to Arjun in the Gita – "**Sukh dukhe samey kritva labha labhojaya jayo.**" Meaning, that a human being whose mind remains the same in loss-profit, happiness-sorrow, only he gets peace.

"**Happiness comes from the world, peace comes from within. Happiness is momentary, peace is eternal. You have to pay the price of happiness. Peace is invaluable. It is yours. Sorrow is standing behind happiness. But, behind peace there is only peace.**" In happiness or sorrow, in profit or loss, the human being should pray for this peace only. Consider God's will to be supreme. If God has given me this disease, then there must be some desire of God behind this. If he has made me sit on a throne, then also behind this, he has some desire. When you have surrendered everything to God, then you should be happy in the will of God. It is the work of God to take care of the human beings. He gets the happiness of a mother in doing this work. If the being has a desire behind the service, then he does not get peace out of this service. Sometimes, emotional turmoil comes into his mind, he becomes excited and service also becomes painful.

In the last couplet, the doubt that the devotees had put before the guru, that has been resolved. The guru has explained 'navdha bhakti' (ninefold path of devotion) in these nine couplets. Wealth, family, body, society all these trouble the human being. "**To think is to worry.**" On reaching the fourth state of blessedness, the great men don't indulge in doubts or worry. Doubts and worry are like the waves of an ocean. Till there are waves, there is no peace.

No one has tied you in this world. You have yourself tied yourself by a rope called ego. If this ego is removed, then you are free. Don't consider this life a burden. God is ready to do your welfare. "**Kutshchinta bhavan.**" Meaning, why worry, then? Nothing belonged to you, you had not brought anything with yourself. You are not going to leave anything, then why worry? The present life has become dominated by lust and wealth. Due to this, life has become more focused towards fulfilling your desires. Due to these luxuries, desire is awakened. Pain and disease enter into this life. Pain and disease are both chains, which bind the soul. Sin is born from them. A bitterness comes into the nature. Due to this bitterness, sin arises. Today, religion and the desire for 'moksha' have gone away from human life. Nobody worries about religion. Nobody has any knowledge of religion. Wherever you see, desire and disease is there. Wealth is being wasted to satisfy the senses. This is a waste of life.

The guru told the disciple the path of release from the pain caused by wealth, body, and desire. He told them the medicine for worry – **Krishna ev gatimarmam** (Krishna will worry for you). Wherever I am, in whatever circumstances I am, as long as

I live, I should have one goal and one objective, "**To take shelter under God's benevolent shade.**" This is the opinion of the guru. With the acceptance of the guru, the opinion becomes a principle. Principle is that which is according to the tenets of the scriptures, which is reasonable, which has the blessings of the saints. "**The saints don't talk about the book, they talk about emotion.**" The best knowledge is that which is gained by experience. The knowledge of Kabir was gained by experience, so it used to influence the heart of the people. The guru has said that this is my opinion. This is not his opinion, this is the opinion of a great man. The opinion of a great man means a pure mind, a mind that is dedicated to God. The thoughts that come into the mind of a great man are put there by God Himself.

Till the eighth couplet, the guru told the reasons for worry. Then he told its solution. Constant remembrance of God frees you from worry. Have unbreakable faith in God. You can have faith on him only when you know about his form. By being in good company and by listening to discourses, you come to know about the nature and form of God.

Ved Vyas has clarified the nature and form of God by saying–

"**Sachidananad rupaya vishwotpatyadi he tave**
Tapatraya vinashaaya shrikrishnaya vayam numah."

Meaning, he is the confluence of truth, eternity and bliss. He is the reason for the creation of the world. He is capable of removing the three types of pain. He is Himself the incarnation of bliss. He will give you bliss also. God is never sad. Yes, when the devotees cry due to being separated from Him, then He also remains awake due to the separation pangs, as he used to be troubled by the separation pangs due to His love for the 'gopis'. He demonstrates this feeling for the benefit of the devotees only. If God did not do this, then how will the human beings love Him? So, a being can become free of worry only by thinking about God with a guileless mind and by thinking about Him continuously. The great man reminds the human being that the reason for worry in your life is only this that you have forgotten God. So, you are worried due to the memory of the family, body, society. Dave ji, remember God with a pure feeling daily. See, people do it today in this machine age, but they do not do it with complete devotion. Even the Vedantists and the logicians have accepted this that if God is somewhere, then remembering His name will only benefit you, otherwise there is no harm in taking God's name. But, don't do like this. You do it with complete faith, only then will it be possible. The body has been born from eight natural elements ('Ashtadhaprakriti'). You cannot separate it from nature, so immerse it in the service of the family and the society. But, your soul is not of this nature. It is a part of God. So, immerse it in God. The soul and God belong to the same category. The body and soul belong to different categories. Only people of the same category can come together. People of different categories cannot come together. Like milk and sugar belong to the same category, so even if their form is different, sugar mixes into milk. But, however much you may try to mix stone into milk, it will not mix into it. "**So, the union of the soul and the world is never possible.**" The union of the soul is possible only with God. You don't have to leave the world and run. "**To wear the dress of a sage is easy, but to adopt the qualities of a sage is difficult.**" If the mind has not renunciated the world, then there is no use in wearing the dress of a sage. If your behaviour is that of a sage even while you are living the life of a householder, then you are a sage in white clothes. When this feeling is strengthened that nothing belongs to me, then all worry and turmoil will be quietened. The human beings have formed a relationship with luxuries. Turmoil comes as a result of this. Human beings know how to get into trouble, they don't know how to get out of that trouble. They know how to tie a knot, they don't know how to unravel that knot. The intelligent person is one who doesn't tie the knot in the first place. So, keep your mind focussed on God constantly. So, what do we have to do daily? – **Shri Krishna sharnam mam**. You don't have to go anywhere else except going to the Lord. Salute all celestial Gods, don't disregard anyone, don't oppose anyone, because all of them are a form of God. If you have anger and resentment against someone, then your mind will be upset. Our devotees who follow the 'pushti' method of devotion say some things about Lord Shiva, whereas Vallabhacharya has no opposition to Lord Shiva. Vallabhacharya has considered Shiva to be the guru of the devotees. So, recite the eight-lettered mantra "**Shri Krishna sharnam mam**" daily. The great men have analysed every single letter of this mantra. Otherwise, the main thing in this is the name of God. What is the name of God?

"**Krishibhurvachat shabd anshch nivriti vachakah**
Tyoraikya parbrahama vaishnav ityamidhiyatey."

Meaning, 'Krish' means eternal and 'an' means bliss. 'Krishna' means eternal bliss. So, the one who is Himself the incarnation of bliss, only He can give you bliss. There is bliss in suffering the separation pangs of God also. Ask Chaitanaya Mahaprabhu if he is sad. Ask Meera the bliss of crying. You worldly people cry for money, and feel it is correct to do so. But, if someone cries for God, then he is foolish! You don't know the bliss in this. Like if a worm who lives in cow dung, is removed from the cow dung and bathed in the water of the Ganga and kept on a sweetmeat, he will die. It is able to live in cow dung only. So, God is eternal bliss and only he can give you eternal bliss.

"**Bhaktanam papadidoshan nivaryati**
karshyati iti Krishnaah."

Meaning, one who removes the faults of the devotees. If you have dedicated everything to him, then he will remove your sins. This does not mean that you have got a licence to commit sins. No, it is not so. But, ask forgiveness from God for sins committed unknowingly. Otherwise, he is 'one who has all the good qualities', he is fully capable. He can do everything for you. You just pray to him-

Karji karjo beda paar kanhaiya tharo che adhar
Natwar nand ji na ho lal kanhaiya tharo che adhar
Mahari dagmag dole naiya aney paar karo ney kanhaiya
Parja parja china taar kanhaiya tharo che adhar.
Natwar nand.....

Ekey chidey naiya doobey padti jad mein jainey doobey
Oochey asha to ik taar kanhaiya tharo che adhar
Natwar nad ji.....
Shrinath ji sutan haath na dharjo mahari
naiya nirmal kar do
Tamo che bhav jal taran har kanhaiya tharo che adhar
Natwar nand.......
Har dam naam Tamara laiye namey utarey bhav jal paar
Kanhaiya tharo chey adhar
Natwar......
Bhakta tujhne bhajta rahe che vaishnav
thare bharose rahey che
Aavo aavo mahare dwar kanhaiya tharo che adhar
Natwar....
Karjo karjo.....

The great guru is saying that if God will take away our sins, then the question comes, "Why does God make us commit sins, in the first place? God, why do you bind us in lust, anger, greed in the first place? Why don't you keep us away from these bad habits?" Understand one thing, here nothing is a bad habit. It is human beings who have made good qualities into bad qualities due to their foolishness. Lust is essential for the creation of the world. Anger is also essential, but anger should not be uncontrollable, it should be within limits. To give in to anger without thinking is wrong. To punish someone appropriately, by peaceful and carefully thought out anger is correct. Greed has its own place. Manu Maharaj has said that we should save 20% of our income for the future. Otherwise, the more greedy a person is, the bigger donor he is because he does not spend anything on himself. In the end, he leaves everything here and goes away. Even Bali will become ashamed in front of such a donor. So, to use lust and anger judiciously in life is also a good quality. We have made them into bad qualities. God will free you from sins, he will free you from the habit of committing sins. O brothers and sisters, if you will chant the name of God at all times, then your habit of committing sins will cease. The habit of chanting the name of

God, makes you leave the habit of committing sins. Second thing, by chanting the name of God, the grip of desire becomes weaker. The bonds of attachment break. Your ordinary sight will become divine sight. This world will seem a godly place. By taking the name of God, the strength to bear sorrows increases."

"**The name of God makes you forget your sorrows. To forget your sorrows is to be happy.**" That is why Tulsi Baba has said, "**Tumhare bhajan Ram ko pave, janam janam ke dukh bisrave.**" Meaning, by remembering God's name, you will forget the sorrows that have been plaguing you since many births. Otherwise, the past has no existence, and the future is unknown, the present is in your hands. You have to improve this only. "**Kaal karey so aaj kar.**" Meaning, what you have put off till tomorrow, do today. Sing today the devotional songs that you wanted to sing tomorrow. So, if sorrow comes, remember God's name. You can be successful in devotion only when you are able to conquer your tongue. The tongue entangles you in taste and debate. "**If the tongue is spoilt, the life is spoilt.**" All the drama of the world is due to this only. So, "**by taking the name of God, you are able to conquer your tongue.**" By chanting the name of God, the nature of human beings improves. Nothing has changed in this machine age. Only the nature of human beings has changed. Dattatreya Maharaj said this to Yadu, "Yadu, the reason for the sorrow of human beings is their nature." The great guru says, "**By chanting the name of God, the nature of human beings improves.**" The sight will either see the flower or the thorn. If your nature improves, then your sight will only see the flowers. So, there is only one method of purifying your nature and to make your life a success – **Bhaj man narayan narayan narayan.** Meaning, chant the name of God always.

Jai jai shri radhey – 3
Shri dwarkadheesh ki jai,
Bal Krishna lal ki jai
On namah parvati pataye
Jai jai shri radhe-3

•••

*

"SHRI KRISHNAARPANAM ASTU"

AN OFFERING AT THE LOTUS-FEET OF

LORD SHRI KRISHNA.

*

GLOSSARY

Gopi – Cowherds' daughters
Acharya – Guru, teacher
Maharaj – A term of respect
Ekadashi – The eleventh day in the fortnight of a lunar month
Govind – An epithet of God
Ashtang yoga – A type of yoga
Shuddhadvait – A religious philosophy
Addvaitism – A religious philosophy
Nirvikalp samadhi – A type of meditative state
Indradev – King of heaven
Kaliyug – Machine age; an age in which, according to the Vedas, the importance of religion and goodness will be very low. It is the age of discord, quarrel and striff.
Kshirsagar – White-coloured ocean in which God lives
Mantras – Holy verses
Yagnas – A ritual of worship
Aarti – A ritual in which God is worshipped by keeping lighted earthen lamps, incense sticks, and other materials on a plate and then moving the plate in circles before the idol of God.
Pandit – Priest
Varah avtaar – The incarnation of Lord Vishnu in which he was born as a tortoise
Devta – Celestial beings
Airavat – Elephant of Indra, King of heaven